THE

PERSONAL

STRESS *REDUCTION*

PROGRAM

THE

PERSONAL

STRESS *REDUCTION*

PROGRAM

Dr. Jeffrey W. Forman
DeAnza College

with **Dave Myers**

PRENTICE-HALL, INC., Englewood Cliffs, N.J. 07632

Editorial/production supervision: Shelia Whiting
Cover design: Lundgren Graphics, Ltd.
Manufacturing buyer: Harry P. Baisley

The Publisher offers discounts on this book when ordered
in bulk quantities: For more information write:

   Special Sales/College Marketing
   Prentice-Hall, Inc.
   College Book Division
   Englewood Cliffs, New Jersey 07632
   (201)592-2498

Printed in the United States of America

10 9 8 7 6 5 4 3 2 1

ISBN 0-13-659285-6 01

ISBN 0-13-659277-5 01 (PBK)

Prentice-Hall International (UK) Limited, *London*
Prentice-Hall of Australia Pty. Limited, *Sydney*
Prentice-Hall Canada Inc., *Toronto*
Prentice-Hall Hispanoamericana, S.A., *Mexico*
Prentice-Hall of India Private Limited, *New Delhi*
Prentice-Hall of Japan, Inc., *Tokyo*
Prentice-Hall of Southeast Asia Pte. Ltd., *Singapore*
Editora Prentice-Hall do Brasil, Ltda., *Rio de Janeiro*

This book is dedicated to my wife Kathi, my sons Jared and Myles, and my parents Bernice and Carl. Their love, support, encouragement and belief in me gave me the needed strength during those late nights at the computer.

CONTENTS

INTRODUCTION

Ever since prehistoric beasts chased the first cavemen in search of an easy meal, stress has been with us. Stress is your body's natural "fight or flight" response to threats, challenges, and physical dangers. Today's stresses come from different, more modern sources such as job, family, or just plain survival in a complicated world, but your bodily reactions are the same. If, like our terrified ancestor, you can sprint to the safety of a cave or otherwise find some outlet for the stress, your body returns to its normal relaxed state. Unrelieved stress, on the other hand, keeps you in a state of tension and, just like that hungry beast, will eventually destroy you.

Many people don't know about the safe, healthy, and successful ways of dealing with modern stresses. Too often, people under stress try to artificially escape it through alcohol, drugs (like cocaine and marijuana), muscle relaxants, tranquilizers, and sleeping pills. These sad escapes merely suppress stress symptoms and lead to other serious problems of liver damage, impotence, fatigue, nausea, drowsiness, gastric irritation and bleeding, and mental confusion.

This workbook is about the healthy ways to relieve stress. Of course, you've probably seen a lot of other books on the same topic. What makes this workbook different is that it offers you a *personalized* approach for developing your own unique stress reduction plan and then integrating that plan into your life.

The idea behind this workbook is simple. A series of questionnaires that you fill out in the privacy of your own home will reveal the kinds of stress you're under and how it is affecting you. Answers on the questionnaires define your *Stress Profile*, which is unique to you. Following the questionnaires are descriptions of a whole range of exercises--both physical and mental--that show how to relieve specific problems.

By matching the stresses on the Profile with exercises to relieve them, you build your own personalized stress reduction program. There is also a chart for matching stresses with exercises, but it's only to help guide you in building the program. You're not constrained in any way from trying out any of the exercises. Quite simply, you use the ones that help you relax and feel good. You may not need all of the information in the workbook to combat your own stresses, but be assured that what you do need is here. LET'S GET STARTED.

Acknowledgements

The author would like to extend his gratitude to Kathi Forman for her fine illustrations, to Nathan Myers for his skills as a cartoonist, to Judy Bobos for her word processing prowess, and to Dave Myers for his proficiency with a red pencil.

THE

PERSONAL

STRESS *REDUCTION*

PROGRAM

CHAPTER 1: WHAT IS STRESS AND WHAT DOES IT DO TO YOUR BODY?

Stress is the body's physical, mental, and chemical reaction to circumstances that frighten, excite, confuse, challenge, surprise, anger, endanger, or irritate. The events that cause stress may be good or bad. Good stress (known as eustress) can come from happy events such as job promotions, getting married or becoming a parent. Bad stress (distress) is much more common, coming from such everyday events as unrealistic job deadlines, money worries, and even the grind of daily commuting.

From good to bad, stress is a spectrum. A certain amount of good stress acts as a catalyst for achieving optimum performance, but too much or too little stress (good or bad!) can damage your health and well-being. The list in the following table shows the symptoms of stress underloads and overloads that may progress to physical and mental breakdowns. Where do you fit in this list? Notice that some of the symptoms--like alcoholism--are for underloads and overloads.

Too Little Stress	The Right Amount of Stress	Too Much Stress
Dull thinking	Clear thinking and perception	Cloudy thinking
Irritability	Calmness under duress	Irritability
Decreased motivation	High motivation	Motivated but overloaded
Lethargic performance	Efficient and effective performance	Poor quality performance
Apathy	High energy and expectations	Apathy
Negativity	Effective decision-making and problem analysis	Reduced judgement and recall
More accidents	Excellent memory recall	More accidents
Changing appetite	High creativity	Changing appetite
Erratic interrupted sleep	Normal sleep patterns	Sleep onset insomnia
Increased absenteeism	Work is a positive challenge	Increased absenteeism
More alcohol and drug abuse	Natural Exhilaration	More alcohol and drug abuse
		Chronic fatigue
		Social withdrawal
		Strained relationships
		Decreased creativity

STRESS LOAD SYMPTOMS CHART

STRESS ON THE JOB

Job-related stress and strain have been studied extensively in the last few years. Not surprisingly, researchers found that job stress can severely damage your health if it persists.

Typically, job stress falls into five stages.

In the first stage of job stress people suffer from anxiety, anger, tension, and the general feeling of "being uptight." These feelings occur at the same time the stress itself occurs. For example, when the boss yells at you, chances are you'll feel the first stages of stress.

Step two is the response to chronic stress. The responses are mostly psychological, ranging from constant depression to feelings of fatigue. Continually stressed workers also often complain of alienation and general malaise.

The third stage of job-related stress is when actual physiological changes start to take place. Blood pressure rises, hormone levels and nutrients in the blood become unbalanced and stomach muscles stay constantly tightened.

By the fourth stage physical health actually starts deteriorating. Typical symptoms of this advanced stage of stress include: gastro-intestinal disorders, coronary heart disease, asthmatic attacks, and other psychosomatic problems.

In the fifth and final stage of job-related strain, work performance is degraded, productivity falls drastically and errors creep into all phases of work. By now a worker is more of a detriment than asset to the job and may, because of the reactions to stress, be fired.

What are stressful job situations? Different jobs have different stresses, but they can be summarized in general:

Role Ambiguity - Lack of clarity about the scope and responsibility of a job

Role Conflicts - Forced to do things against better judgment

Long hours - Lack of time for self and family

Excessive travel

Forced relocation

A poor work environment

3

Decision-making

Lack of feedback from supervisors

Inability to get pertinent information and/or adequate equipment and funding to get the job done

Deadlines

Low chances for promotion

Lack of authority

Personal conflicts

Not enough involvement on major decisions

Too much work, or not enough challenge

Low pay

Managers experience additional job stresses (although these stresses aren't limited just to managers):

Two-sided pressure - from above and below

Too few employees to get a job done

High employee absenteeism

High turnover rates

Critical decision-making that involves taking risks

Audits

Personnel problems

Rapidly changing marketplace

Competition from other businesses

Back-stabbing (definitely not limited to managers!)

Labor strikes

Feelings of inadequacy to perform job

THE SPECTRUM OF STRESS

Your Reactions To Stress

You're in line at a bank when suddenly a gunman yells, "everyone down on the floor, this is a stick up." As you prepare for action, your body undergoes the following reactions:

More blood sugars and fats flow to the muscles and brain

Pupils dilate

Heart rate increases

Breathing becomes faster

Many muscles tense and tighten

Blood pressure rises

Stomach and intestines temporarily halt digestion

Muscles controlling the bowels and bladder loosen

Perspiration increases

Blood clotting mechanisms start up

The hormones epinephrine (adrenaline) and norepinephrine pour into the blood

All senses are heightened

But you don't have to be involved in a bank robbery for these reactions to occur. Everyday stress triggers the same kinds of responses as your body prepares to combat any other imposing threat. The problem is that your body pays a price each time it's stressed. And the more intense the stress or the longer it lasts, the higher the price.

The Price You Pay For Stress

Ironically, the fight or flight response itself becomes a major source of distress when fired too often or for too long, causing the body to remain in a state of permanent mobilization. The result is, at best, chronic tension. Worse, the hormones secreted in abundance during the response can weaken the immune system and ultimately damage vital organs or the nervous system itself. This excessive wear and tear produces physical and psychological disorders, premature aging, and even early death.

In fact, an estimated 50 to 80% of all disease in this country have stress related origins. A specific (but by no means exhaustive) list of diseases that may be stress-induced covers you from head to toe:

Migraine Headaches - Headaches due to abnormal blood flow in the arteries of the head.

Bronchial Asthma - Recurrent attacks of shortness of breath and wheezing due to spasming contractions of the lungs.

Coronary Artery Disease - Heart disease.

Paroxysmal Tachycardia - Rapid pounding of the heart that occurs suddenly for no apparent reason.

Atopic Dermatitis - Inflammation and crusting of the skin that may be caused by allergy, heredity, or stress.

Peptic Ulcer - A defect or hole in the lining of the esophagus, stomach, or first portion of the small intestine that is caused by excess digestive acid.

Mucous Colitis - Excess secretion of mucous and spasm in the colon that results in constipation and/or diarrhea with the passage of mucous.

Ulcerative Colitis - The chronic recurrent development of sores in the colon which may result in cramping abdominal pain and bleeding.

Urticaria - Hives.

Amenorrhea - Absence or abnormal stoppage of the menstrual cycle.

Enuresis - Bed wetting.

Impotence - Lack of the ability to maintain erections.

Hyperthyroidism - Excessive activity of the thyroid gland.

Hypertension - High blood pressure.

Raynaud's Disease - Periodic attacks of very poor blood flow to the fingers, toes, and sometimes the ears and nose.

Sleep Onset Insomnia - Difficulty falling to sleep.

Alcoholism - Addiction to alcohol.

Drug Addiction - cocaine, marijuana, barbiturates.

Many neurotic and psychotic disorders.

By the way, even though most research has focused on stresses and strains in the workplace, the same maladies occur in the classroom and home. Any housewife with small children, or any student taking final exams, can readily attest to being under stress.

Have you seen yourself or your job situation in this brief description of stress? Do you suffer from any or all of the symptoms? If so, it's time to do something about it to fight back. Just agreeing to do that is the first step on the road to regaining your physical and mental health.

CHAPTER 2:   HOW TO COMBAT STRESS:
THE PRINCIPLES OF STRESS REDUCTION

Now that you know what stress is, can you fight it? Of course. Here's
what you'll be doing in the rest of this workbook:

Determining the cause of your distress
Finding out where stress is affecting you physically
Developing your own, individual stress reduction plan of action
Putting your plan to work
Sticking to it
Reinforcing relaxing behavior
And relaxing

The first step in overcoming stress is to take an honest, in-depth look at
your physical health, psychological health, and your lifestyle. Getting
your distresses out in the open in this way and then putting them all
down on paper will bring you face to face with the enemy. It's vital that
you be honest and complete when describing the stresses because you'll be
treating them later as a group instead of as fragments.

Your evaluation of stress will show:
What is causing the stress?
Where it is affecting you physically?

7

What you can do to reduce it?

An excellent technique to gain an increased awareness of the causes of stress is to chart your behavior over a typical week. Slip a small notebook into your pocket or purse and carry it with you for a whole week. Whenever you experience a stress reaction write down the time of day, what caused it, and how you physically and mentally reacted to it. Also note if you did anything to reverse the stress (how you coped with it) and if your actions were successful. If you are under stress you'll soon see a pattern developing of the causes and successful cures. Furthermore, a week's worth of stress laid out in black and white should open your eyes to what may be an astonishing number of daily stresses, both large and small. Armed with your new awareness, you're now ready to develop your own personal stress inventory.

DEVELOPING YOUR PERSONAL STRESS INVENTORY

The Personal Stress Inventory (PSI) is a two-part questionnaire that helps you gather all the information necessary to formulate your individual stress reduction strategy. Section 1 of the PSI is about your physical and psychosocial state of being. It summarizes your medical history of stress-related disorders, stress symptoms, medications taken, nutritional habits, stimulants ingested, sleep, exercise and relaxation patterns.

Section 1 also identifies the situations that cause or add to your stress, such as: school, work, family, money, undeterminable anxiety, decision-making, lack of achievement, lack of control over your life, and lack of motivation.

Section 2 is for checking your posture, flexibility, and ability to breathe properly. Often, without you ever knowing about them, these factors contribute to your stress. In addition, Section 2 has questions to determine if you suffer from trigger points (very sensitive spots or knots in muscles) that could be causing pain.

YOUR PERSONAL STRESS INVENTORY

Directions: Set aside a half hour or so to fill out the PSI. You'll need a helper for Section 2. Answer only the questions that pertain to you, but do answer them fully (nobody else will see them). Most important of all, relax. The PSI is *not* another stress in your life.

Section 1

Part A

Do you now or ever have you had? (check those that apply):

Yes No

___ ✓ High blood pressure (hypertension)

___ ✓ Heart trouble

✓ ✓ Colitis (irritated inflamed intestine)

✓ ✓ Ulcer or digestive troubles

___ ✓ Asthma

___ ✓ Cancer

___ ✓ Arthritis

Part B

Using the following scale:

1 – Never   2 – Rarely   3 – Sometimes   4 – Often   5 – Always

To what extent do you experience the following? (circle those that apply):

1 2 ③ 4 5   Sweaty palms

1 2 ③ 4 5   Cold hands and feet

1 2 3 ④ 5   Tension headaches

1 ② 3 4 5   Migraine headaches

1 2 3 4 ⑤   Teeth grinding

1 2 3 4 ⑤   Neck pains

1 2 ③ 4 5   Uncontrollable muscle spasms

1 2 3 4 ⑤   Pains in the shoulder and/or upper back

1 2 3 ④ 5   Low back pain

1 2 ③ 4 5   Pain down the back of your legs

1 2 ③ 4 5   Shortness of breath

1 ② 3 4 5   Susceptibility to minor illness

1 ② 3 4 5   Poor quality sleep

1 2 3 ④ 5   Chronic fatigue

Part C

How frequently do you experience the following? (circle those that apply):

1 2 3 ④ 5   Not enough time in the day

1 2 3 ④ 5   Trouble concentrating (difficulty thinking clearly)

1 2 3 ④ 5   Anxiety due to causes that you cannot pinpoint

1 2 3 ④ 5   Irritability

1 2 ③ 4 5   Strained relationships

1 2 ③ 4 5   Easily aroused hostility

9

1 2 3 4 (5) Job dissatisfaction

1 2 3 (4) 5 Depression

1 (2) 3 4 5 Taking work home with you

1 2 3 (4) 5 Thinking about work even when relaxing

1 2 (3) 4 5 Being a workaholic

1 2 3 (4) 5 Trouble turning off your mind at night

1 2 (3) 4 5 Decision-making anxiety

1 2 (3) 4 5 Stressful dreams

1 2 (3) 4 5 Non-stop rushing around

1 2 3 4 (5) Low motivation

1 2 3 (4) 5 Pessimism

1 2 3 (4) 5 Worrying

1 2 3 (4) 5 Lack of control over your life

1 2 3 (4) 5 A short-fused temper

(1) 2 3 4 5 Functioning subnormally or missing work because of drug or alcohol abuse

Part D

Circle the diet that best describes your eating habits on a typical day?

A. Lots of fruit and vegetables (salads), whole grains and legumes, less than 30% of all consumed comes from fat, at least two glasses of milk products each day, low cholesterol and little sugar. More fish, turkey, and chicken than red meat.

B. Lots of fast food, junk food, soda pop and grease.

C. Meat and potatoes.

D. Vegetarian.

E. A combination of _____ and _____

List the name and dose of any medications you are currently taking (including appetite suppressants and vitamin pills):

Vit. C + B

Estimate the number of cups of stimulants you drink each day (coffee, tea, soft drinks): ___4___

Do you practice some form of deep relaxation (such as meditation) for at least twenty minutes, three times a week? Yes (No)

Do you participate in vigorous non-stop physical activities that elevate your heart rate for at least twenty minutes, three times a week? Yes (No)

10

What time of the day do you feel most stressed? What happens at these times (i.e. commute traffic or the daily meeting with the boss)? Use more paper if necessary. *Work - home late after noon*
muscle tension upper back & neck
muscle aches, low motivation, fatigue

The following factors are common contributors to stress. Put them in the order that you think they contribute to your stress level. Put a 1 next to the element that causes the most stress, then a 2 next to your second biggest stressor, and so on down the list.

1	Job/Studies
4	Family
5	Social/Sexual
2	Financial
3	Health
	(Other) _____

List three or more lifestyle changes that you think may improve the quality of your life.
diet
exercise
meditation

List some ideas for coping with, or eliminating, your stressors. Include even the most bizarre alternatives that you can imagine. Don't inhibit your creativity.
meditation
floating tank
reading

Section 2

Directions: You need a helper with a wrist watch or stop watch to complete this section of your PSI. Some of the evaluations are done while you're lying down, so clear a comfortable place on the floor. Also, dress casually or even wear a swim suit because your helper will need to check certain groups of your muscles.

Part 2A

Posture Evaluation

Check the picture that most closely resembles your posture. Often, poor posture indicates stress, while simultaneously contributing to it.

11

Forward Head

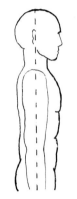 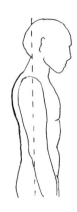 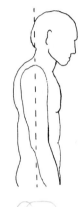

Normal Posture   Mild   Severe

Round Shoulders

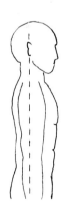  

Normal Posture   Mild   Severe

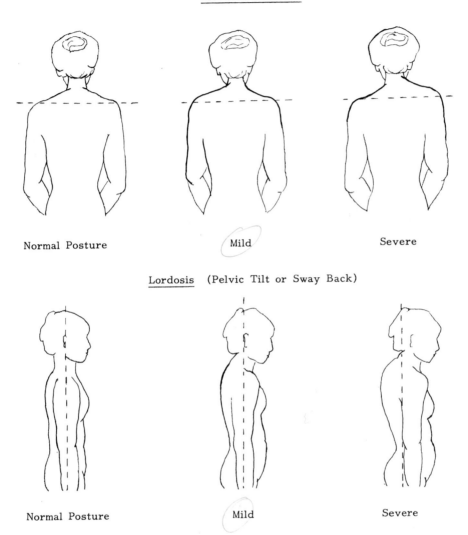

Elevated Shoulder

Normal Posture   Mild   Severe

Lordosis (Pelvic Tilt or Sway Back)

Normal Posture   Mild   Severe

Part 2B

Flexibility Evaluation

Excess tightness in muscles can cause poor posture, pain, and fatigue, as well as joint and skeletal problems. Have your helper look closely at the following muscle groups and check their lengths compared to the illustrations.

13

Hip Flexors

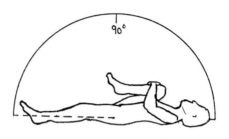

Normal Length

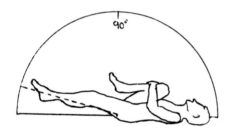

Mild Shortness

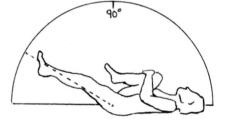

Severe

Quadriceps (thighs)

Normal Length

14

Mild Shortness

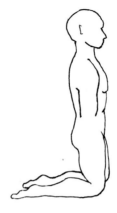

Severe

Low Back Muscles

Normal Length

Mild Shortness

Severe

Hamstring

Normal Length

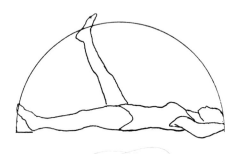

Mild Shortness

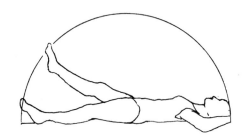

Severe

Calves

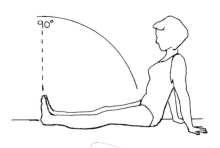

Normal Length

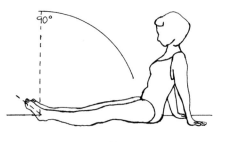

Severe

16

Hip Adductors (on insides of thighs)

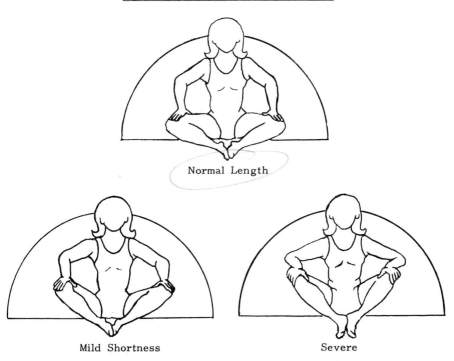

Normal Length

Mild Shortness

Severe

Try to assume the positions illustrated below. If you can't, don't strain. Have your helper circle (right on the illustrations) the appropriate positions you can comfortably attain.

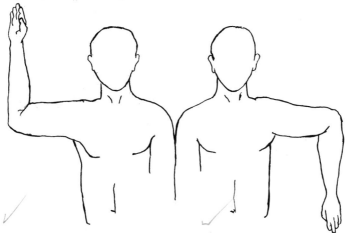

Normal Shoulder External Rotation

Normal Shoulder Internal Rotation

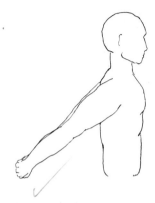

Normal Shoulder Flexion   Normal Shoulder Hyperextension

Part 2C

Muscle Tension Evaluation

Severe stress frequently produces very tender points in some of your muscles. These bands of muscle tension are called trigger points or knots. Sensitive knots can cause localized or radiating pain that can lead to a variety of problems. Have your helper press on each point shown on the drawings below. Circle the points that are only slightly painful, draw an X on those that are very painful. (Activities described later on show how to eliminate the pain points.)

 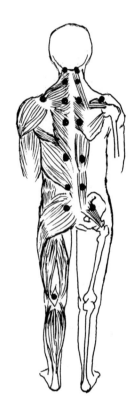

Front   Back

Part 2D

Breathing Evaluation

The way you breathe is a good indicator of your state of stress. By
evaluating five breathing factors you can tell if stress has interrupted
your body's oxygen intake and waste gas elimination. The five factors
are:

19

Length of inhalation

Length of exhalation

Shoulder elevation

Action of the diaphragm

Overall control

Sit or lie down and relax. Have your helper get the stop watch or wrist watch ready to measure your breathing rate. You'll be measuring the time it takes to inhale and exhale. Also, your helper needs to observe the way you breathe. Read the next four questions that tell what to look for. Now, take in a long, slow, deep breath through your nose. Breathe in as slowly as possible. Record the time it takes to inhale. Release the breath, exhaling through your nose as slowly as possible. Record the exhale time. Do it again and record the times for the second breath too.

Trial 1 (Time)   Trial 2 (Time)

    Inhalation _____   Inhalation_____

    Exhalation_____   Exhalation_____

1. Do your shoulders move when you breathe?   YES____   NO_✓_

2. Does your lower ribs and belly button
    push out when you began to take air in?   YES_✓_   NO____

3. Does your breath in travel from the
    bottom to the top of your chest?   YES____   NO_✓_

4. Does your breathing feel deep, relaxed,
    and coordinated?   YES____   NO_✓_

This completes your PSI. By merely filling it in you should have a much clearer picture of the causes and symptoms of your stress. The rest of this workbook tells you how to relieve the stresses.

CHAPTER 3: DEVELOPING AN ANTI-STRESS PLAN

You have now come to the gates of good health. Believe it or not, this is where many people falter. They've learned about stress, met it, shook its hand and now think that's all there is to getting rid of it. Not true. If you turn back now you'll allow stress to destroy your life and health. Now is the time to grab your life back from stress. How? By reducing the effects of the unchecked tension, dangerous hormonal changes and cloudy thinking that accompany stress. Success may involve changes to your diet, job, academic major, exercise patterns, and even living situations. Know this from the start: No wonder drug can eliminate your stress and no one else can do it but you. If you don't change your life to eliminate your stress-related problems, the painful consequences will happen just as sure as the sun sets each day.

First, re-read your PSI to pinpoint the major causes of your stress. Next, sit quietly and think about the parts of your body that you've identified as being painful or tense. Now, tune into your emotional feelings about your life's stresses. Soon you'll begin to see clearly what the stresses are and what they are doing to your body. Pain especially is an indication that something is wrong; don't suppress stress symptoms with drugs, instead get to the root of your physical problems.

Likewise, anxiety and depression are indications that something is

21

interfering with your peace of mind. Let your mind pinpoint the causes of your stress. With the above in mind, you can now complete your personal stress plan.

WHAT TO DO WITH THE PSI DATA?

The PSI has put your personal stress profile on paper. Its results outline your history of stress related problems, the factors that cause or contribute to your stress, and information about how stress is affecting you physically and psychologically. This valuable data is all the information you need to map out your personal stress reduction plan. The following guidelines explain how to match your PSI results with the stress reduction reference chart listed below. As you match the stresses revealed on your PSI with the specific stress reduction techniques in the rest of this book, you are creating your own personal stress management plan.

The stress reduction reference chart shows specific recommendations for each problem area uncovered by your PSI. Stresses or problems are cross-referenced to the chapters and techniques that will specifically help you cope more successfully.

How To Use Your PSI Results
Section 1

<u>Part 1A</u>   Circle all the PSI yes responses on the stress reduction reference chart. Also circle the corresponding reference sections listed in the chart's right hand column.

<u>Part 1B and 1C</u>   All 1 and 2 responses indicate that you are coping successfully. Relax and keep it that way.

All 3 responses indicate that you periodically have stress problems. Although the stresses are not yet chronic you should learn techniques for coping more successfully to prevent the conditions from worsening. On the chart, find and circle all the 3 responses.

All 4 and 5 responses are danger signals that you have chronic stress problems. You must learn to cope more successfully and reverse the negative effects of your stress before it takes a severe toll on your health and longevity. Circle all the factors that you scored a 4 or 5 on and highlight them (with a checkmark or star). Don't sit back now; you must take action against these symptoms.

Part D   All PSI responses are covered in the reference chart.   Find your response and circle the corresponding sections to read.

Section 2

Circle the problems you have and the recommended stress reduction techniques.

STRESS REDUCTION REFERENCE CHART

Problems	Stress Reduction Techniques	Chapter(s)
	Section 1 / Part A	
High blood pressure	Controlled breathing, flexibility and aerobic exercises, deep relaxation, and diet	4, 5, 6, 7, 10
Heart trouble	Controlled breathing, aerobic and flexibility exercises, deep relaxation, and diet	4, 5, 6, 7, 10
Colitis	Deep relaxation (visual imagery) and breathing exercises	4, 7
Ulcer or digestive troubles	Controlled breathing, aerobic exercise and deep relaxation (visual imagery)	4, 5, 7
Asthma	Breathing mechanics, abdominal strengthening exercises, posture and stretching exercises	4, 5, 6
Cancer	Controlled breathing, flexibility and aerobic exercise, deep relaxation (visual imagery) and pain control	4, 5, 6, 7, 9
Arthritis	Flexibility and posture improvement and pain control	5, 6, 9
	Section 1 / Part B	
Sweaty palms	Aerobic and flexibility exercises, controlled breathing, and deep relaxation	4, 5, 6, 7

23

Problems	Stress Reduction Techniques	Chapter(s)
Cold hands and feet	Controlled breathing, aerobic and flexibility exercises, posture and stress, and deep relaxation	4, 5, 6, 7
Severe headaches (tension and migraine)	Controlled breathing, posture improvement, deep relaxation, diet, and pain control (headache relief tips)	4, 6, 7, 9, 10
Teeth grinding	Deep relaxation (muscle tension reduction), pain control (face massage and headache relief tips), and sleep improvement	7, 8, 9
Neck pains	Posture improvement, exercises to avoid, pain control (massage, heat and ice), sleep improvement (pillow recommendations), deep relaxation (muscle awareness and tension relaxation training)	5, 6, 7, 8, 9
Uncontrollable muscle spasms	Posture improvement, deep relaxation (muscle awareness and tension reduction training), pain control (massage, heat and ice), diet and sleep improvement	6, 7, 8, 9, 10
Pains in the shoulder and/or upper back	Posture improvement, pain control (ice, heat, massage and acupressure), deep relax training, and sleep improvement (mattress and pillow recommendations)	6, 7, 8, 9
Low back pain and pain down the back of the legs	Posture improvement and low back exercises, exercises to avoid, back care tips, pain control (ice, heat, massage and acupressure), muscle awareness and relaxation training, and sleep improvement (mattress recommendations)	5, 6, 7, 8, 9
Shortness of breath	Controlled breathing, abdominal strengthening exercises	4, 5
Susceptibility to minor illness	Diet, deep relaxation, and sleep improvement	7, 8, 10
Poor quality sleep	Sleep improvement, diet, deep relaxation training and exercises that reduce stress	5, 7, 8, 10

Problems	Stress Reduction Techniques	Chapter(s)
Chronic fatigue	Sleep improvement, posture improvement, deep relaxation (visual imagery), diet, and aerobic exercise	5, 6, 7, 8, 10

Section 1 / Part C

Problems	Stress Reduction Techniques	Chapter(s)
Not enough time in the day	Time management, making lifestyle changes	11
Trouble concentrating (difficulty thinking clearly	Deep relaxation training, unclouding your thoughts	7, 11
Anxiety due to causes you cannot pinpoint	Coping with psychological and social stress, deep relaxation training	7, 11
Irritability	Coping with psychological and social stress, deep relaxation training	7, 11
Strained relationships	Coping with psychological and social stress, deep relaxation training	7, 11
Easily aroused hostility	Coping with psychological and social stress, deep relaxation training	7, 11
Job dissatisfaction	Job and lifestyle changes	11
Depression	Deep relaxation training (visual imagery), coping with psychological and social stress	7, 11
Taking work home with you	Sleep improvement, using time more effectively, general stress reduction tips	8, 11
Thinking about work even when relaxing	Deep relaxation training (visual imagery), sleep improvement, using time more effectively, and general stress reduction tips	7, 8, 11
Being a workaholic	Deep relaxation training, using time more effectively, general stress reduction tips	7, 11

Problems	Stress Reduction Techniques	Chapter(s)
Trouble turning off the mind at night	Sleep improvement, deep relaxation, diet, controlled breathing, and general stress reduction tips	4, 7, 8, 9, 11
Decision-making anxiety	Effective decision making	11
Stressful dreams	Sleep improvement, controlled breathing, coping with psychological and social stress	4, 8, 11
Non-stop running around	Deep relaxation, using time more effectively	4, 11
Low motivation	Coping with psychological and social stress	11
Pessimism	Coping with psychological and social stress	11
Worrying	Coping with psychological and social stress	11
Lack of control over your life	Coping with psychological and social stress	11
A short-fused	Coping with psychological and social stress	11
Missing work or functioning sub-normally because of drug or alcohol abuse	Coping with psychological and social stress, general stress reduction tips	11

Section 1 / Part D

Diet A	You should teach a class in nutrition	
Diet B	The stress reduction diet	10
Diet C	The stress reduction diet	10
Diet D	The stress reduction diet	10
Diet E	The stress reduction diet	10

Problems	Stress Reduction Techniques	Chapter(s)
Medications taken	Borrow (from the library) a physician's desk reference, or any similar book that lists medications, their uses and potential side effects. Look up the medications that you are taking. Compare your list of stress symptoms to the possible side effects of your medication to see if any relationship exists. If the two lists are similar, inform your doctor about your findings. Your medications may actually be the cause of some of your problems. Under no circumstances should you discontinue taking your medication without the consent of your physician.	
More than one cup of stimulant per day	General tips for reducing food induced stress	10
Yes, I relax 20 minutes 3 times each week	Don't stop	
No, I don't relax 20 minutes 3 times each week	Controlled breathing, deep relaxation training, general stress reduction tips	4, 7, 11
Yes, I raise my heart rate for 20 minutes about 3 times a week	You are strengthening your heart and burning off excess tension so keep up this most beneficial behavior	5
No, I don't raise my heart rate for 20 minutes about 3 times a week	Aerobic training tips	11
The time of day you feel most stressed	Reducing your stress	
Rank order your stressors	Reducing your stress	11

Problems	Stress Reduction Techniques	Chapter(s)
1		
2		
3		
4		
5		
6		

List three or more lifestyle changes that may improve the quality of your life and list your ideas for coping with or eliminating your stressors. Include even the most bizarre alternatives.	Reducing your stress	11

Section 2

Section 2A   Posture Evaluation

Compare your posture to the pictures listed in the PSI. Any deviations from the normal indicate that you have muscular imbalances and need to improve your posture in these areas.	Neck realignment exercises, exercises to reduce round shoulders, low back exercises	6

Section 2B   Flexibility Evaluation

Compare your flexibility to the pictures listed in the PSI. Any deviations from normal indicate short muscles that must be stretched.	Hip flexor stretches, thigh stretches low back stretches, hamstring stretches, calf stretches, hip adductor stretches, shoulder stretches	6

28

Problems	Stress Reduction Techniques	Chapter(s)

Section 2C Muscle Tension Evaluation

Study the painful points on your muscles that you discovered in the PSI. These points indicate excess muscle tension.	Focused breathing, deep relaxation training (muscle tension reduction), pain control (massage, heat, ice and biofeedback)	4, 7, 9

Section 2D Breathing Evaluation

The following pattern is considered normal on this test: Your inhalation lasts at least six seconds and your exhalation lasts at least two seconds longer, or at least eight seconds; the shoulders do not move during inhalation or exhalation, the breath in begins in the diaphragm (a dome shaped muscle a few inches above your belly button) and then progresses to the top of your chest. Your breathing should feel deep, relaxed, and coordinated.

If you do not inhale for at least six seconds, your lung capacity is too small. Read Chapter 4, Controlled Breathing: The Key to Relaxation, and study the mechanics of proper breathing.

If your exhalation is not two seconds longer than your inhalation, your exhalation is too short	Study the mechanics of proper breathing included in the chapter on controlled breathing	4
If your shoulders moved when you breathed, you demonstrated unnecessary shoulder movement that disrupts proper breathing mechanics and may lead to neck and shoulder pain	Study the mechanics of proper breathing included in the chapter on controlled breathing	4

Problems	Stress Reduction Techniques	Chapter(s)
If your in-halation did not begin with your abdomen and lower ribs pushing out, you demonstrated a breathing flaw that can inhibit your ability to breathe efficiently and relax at will	Study the mechanics of proper breathing included in the chapter on controlled breathing	4
If your breathing does not feel deep, relaxed, and coordinated	Study the mechanics of proper breathing included in the chapter on controlled breathing	4

You've finished with the reference chart. Look back through it, at all the circled items and chapters to read. That is your stress reduction plan.

Now that you know what to do, fit the exercises and other stress reduction techniques into your daily schedule. Make certain the schedule is compatible and doesn't cause any problems. For example, schedule your stretching, breathing, and relaxation exercises for Monday, Wednesday, and Friday; and your aerobic exercises for Tuesday, Thursday, and Saturday.

Your next step is to put your plan into action with high energy and great expectations. Then stick to your plan, reinforce your proper behavior, and enjoy the benefits that a healthier, less stressful, lifestyle has to offer.

CHAPTER 4: CONTROLLED BREATHING:
THE KEY TO RELAXATION

If you can voluntarily control your breathing, you can easily learn to calm
your mind and body to relax at any time and at any place. Unfortunately,
many people lack conscious control over their breathing, and breathe
incorrectly.

You breathe about 23,000 times each day. When calm, your breathing is
slow, deep, smooth and regular, but when stressed, your breaths become
quicker, shallower, and demand excess muscular energy (particularly in
the neck and shoulder muscles). Physical problems directly attributed to
improper breathing patterns include headaches, neck, shoulder, and back
pain, poor circulation, hypertension, asthma, hyperventilation, and
insomnia.

THE MECHANICS OF PROPER BREATHING

Proper breathing is a smooth, coordinated progression of movements that
starts in the dome-shaped diaphragm muscle, the principle muscle of
respiration. As shown in the illustration, during inhalation the
diaphragm[1] flattens, allowing more room for the lungs to expand in the
chest cavity. Simultaneously, the abdominal area just above the
bellybutton[2] pushes out. Next, the lower ribs[3] spread as the inhalation progresses from the bottom to the middle of the chest. Finally,

your inhalation ends when the upper ribs[4] elevate and separate, allowing the top of the lungs to expand and fill.

During a normal exhalation, the diaphragm relaxes and resumes its normal dome shape while the lower abdomen and ribs move back to their initial positions, forcing air out. The abdominals and the latissimus dorsi (the large muscle that covers the lower two thirds of the back) are also important muscles of exhalation. Contracting these muscles helps force stale air out of the lungs. This allows greater oxygen exchange and can help to relax you. Your shoulders should remain stationary throughout the entire breathing cycle.

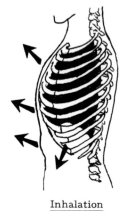

Inhalation   Exhalation

Are you breathing properly? To check if you are, place a hand over your abdomen and watch the movements of your chest. Compare those movements with the illustrations of proper breathing. Concentrate on breathing slowly, smoothly, fully and with the best mechanics possible. Try to breathe through your nose and fill your lungs to capacity. Exhale completely to force most of the air out of your lungs before your next breath.

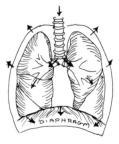

Inhalation

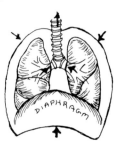

Exhalation

32

COMMON BREATHING FAULTS

The most common breathing faults are:

Poor rhythm - breathing is uncoordinated and does not flow in the proper sequence.

Breathing too shallowly and rapidly; expanding only the upper chest - can lead to an inadequate supply of oxygen to the brain and muscles and possibly to hyperventilation, blackouts and asthma.

Elevating the shoulders - shoulder action is not needed to breathe properly; it can lead to headaches and pains in the neck, shoulders, and upper back.

Over-inflated lungs - Having a barrel chest along with weak abdominal and back muscles can prevent you from exhaling completely (the major problem of asthmatics); if you have this problem you may find that even slight exertion causes respiratory distress (gasping for a deep breath but not having any room for it).

BREATHING AS A RELAXATION TOOL

Learning proper breathing is a giant step toward learning how to successfully cope with stress and tension. Two kinds of breathing -- deep breathing and focused breathing--unlock an innate, in-bred, natural relaxation mechanism that exactly reverses the damaging physiological changes to your body caused by prolonged, unchecked stress. Focused breathing in particular helps calm your mind and body, reduces muscle tension and blood pressure, and counteracts the dangerous chemical and hormonal changes that are characteristic components of prolonged stress.

The following breathing exercises develop the proper technique of slow, steady, smooth, relaxed, controlled breathing. To practice these breathing exercises, find a quiet, warm room, and either sit on a comfortable chair or lie on a rug or mat. Dress in loose, comfortable clothes. (Later, after becoming proficient in the exercises, you can practice them at any time and place you need to relax.)

Basic Deep Breathing Exercises

These four basic exercises will increase your lung capacity and breathing control. Progress as you feel your lung capacity and control increasing. Also, remember that exhalations are always longer than inhalations.

Exercise 1   Breathe in 4 seconds through nose, exhale 6 seconds through nose. Repeat three times. Progress by increasing the time of inhalation and exhalation. Always exhale for at least two seconds longer than you inhale.

Exercise 2   Place thumb over right nostril and breathe in through the left nostril for 4 seconds, then reverse and exhale through the right nostril for 6 seconds while blocking the left nostril. Repeat three times on each side. Progress by increasing the time of inhalation and exhalation. Exhale for at least two seconds longer than you inhale.

Exercise 3   Inhale 4 seconds through the nose and exhale 6 seconds through the mouth, either through pursed lips or by making a hissing sound. Repeat three times. Progress by increasing the time of inhalation and exhalation. Exhale for at least two seconds longer than you inhale.

Exercise 4   Inhale 6 seconds through the nose. Hold the breath for 6 seconds while relaxing your mind and entire body. (This pause in breathing is deeply relaxing.) Exhale as slowly as you can for at least 8 seconds. Progress by increasing the time for inhalation, pause, and exhalation.

During these exercises, it may help you to listen to soft music or silently repeat the following key words or suggestions:

My whole body feels peaceful and relaxed.
I feel limp and loose, relaxed and comfortable.
My body feels limp like a rag doll.
I feel like a balloon that has just been punctured.
I feel like butter melting in a frying pan.
My chest and abdomen feel warm and heavy.

Focused Breathing Exercises

Once you're comfortable with deep breathing, you can begin the focused breathing techniques. These advanced breathing techniques induce deep relaxation by having you concentrate on the breathing process itself. The total concentration in these exercises helps you to relax and relieve your stresses because it forces you to STOP thinking about your problems. Constantly dwelling on negative thoughts and worries, even when supposedly relaxing, is a major plague of the highly stressed. If you have these kinds of destructive thought patterns, focused breathing techniques will help you break them and deeply relax at will.

You'll need a tape recorder to practice focused breathing at first. Don't try to do the exercises by simply reading the following instructions; you just can't concentrate enough that way. Instead, record the instructions by reading them out loud. Speak slowly and evenly, preferably when you're reasonably relaxed. If you try to make the recording while stressed, your voice will be tense and high-pitched reminding you of the very same stresses you're trying to defeat. If you don't want to go through the rigamorole of taping these instructions, you can order pre-recorded cassettes. See the last page of this workbook.

When the recording is as you want it, you're ready to start learning focused breathing. Wearing loose clothes, sit on or lie down in a warm, quiet place. Turn on the recorder, close your eyes, and follow the instructions.

Instructions for Focused Breathing: *To begin, take a long, slow, deep, relaxing, complete breath in through your nose and when you are ready exhale as slowly and fully as you possibly can through your nose. Place all of your conscious awareness on your breathing. Turn off all unnecessary thoughts, tune out all distracting noises, and silence your internal voice.*

Continue to breathe slowly, smoothly, and quietly. In your mind, picture fresh, clean oxygen-rich air flowing through your nose and passing through your throat and chest until it reaches your lungs. Picture and feel your lungs expanding to their maximum and then emptying totally like large pink balloons filling completely and then collapsing totally when empty.

When you inhale, feel your belly button push out and your lower ribs separate. Feel your breath filling the bottom, the middle, and finally the top of your lungs. When you exhale, feel all the muscles in your body, from the top of your head to the tip of your toes, totally relax. Feel loose and limp, warm and heavy, deeply...deeply relaxed.

Now, think of nothing but the movement of air within yourself. Remember that each breath is nourishing your entire body with fresh oxygen-rich blood, and each exhalation is cleansing your body. If your thoughts stray from your breathing, bring them back and focus your entire awareness on your breathing. Continue to concentrate on your breathing until you hear my voice again. (At this point in recording these instructions, let the recorder run for 5 to 10 minutes without speaking, then read the next sentence.) *When I count to three, you'll open your eyes and feel much better than before; your eyesight will be improved, your reaction time quicker, your blood pressure lower, and your heart rate slowed down. You will feel totally relaxed and refreshed. One - Two - Three; Eyes Open.*

Now fast-forward the tape to the end of the first side, take it out of the machine and flip it over. You'll be recording this next exercise on Side 2 of the tape. Record as before. When you're ready to practice the exercise, get comfortable, close your eyes, turn on the recorder and follow the instructions.

To begin, take a long, slow, deep complete breath through your nose. Hold the breath for a short, comfortable pause and, when you are ready, exhale it through your nose as slowly and as fully as you possibly can. Repeat three times. Continue relaxed breathing and focus all of your awareness on it. Now count your breaths from one to ten. When you reach 10, count back down to one. If you lose count, don't worry, simply return to the number one and start again. (Give yourself about ten minutes for this part.)

Now, focus your concentration on a point an inch below your navel. Feel it rise with each inhalation and fall with each exhalation. Feel gravity pulling you down. Let all the weight of your body go, giving in to the force of gravity. Feel your entire body totally relax more and more with each breath.

When I count to three, you'll open your eyes and feel much better than before. When you open your eyes you will still be totally relaxed, but awake and alert so that you can enjoy your wonderful feeling of total relaxation. One - Two - Three; Eyes Open.

CHAPTER 5: EXERCISES THAT REDUCE STRESS

The human body is a sophisticated machine that must be exercised regularly to keep running properly. If you aren't active or don't exercise, your muscles (heart included) will shrink and grow weak, endurance falls, bones grow soft, fat deposits accumulate, flexibility decreases, blood chemistry changes, muscle tension builds up, posture deteriorates, and you will age quickly.

Conversely, exercise reduces depression and anxiety, improves sleep quality, burns off muscle tension and calories, provides a great mental release, and may reduce blood pressure (not every exercise does this). Furthermore, you may eventually experience the exercise-induced euphoria, known as the runner's high, that is a natural tension reliever.

It's never too late to begin exercising. The President's Council on Physical Fitness and Sports concluded that exercise can help to achieve significant improvements in strength, endurance, flexibility, coordination, and balance even for those people who have been sedentary for many years. However, some common-sense advice: before you go out and join a health spa or run the Boston marathon, consider the following activities that should be avoided or tried gently, if at all. Better to use the safer alternatives.

Activities to Avoid, or Use with Caution:	Safer Alternatives:

Activities to Avoid, or Use with Caution:

Neck Rolling or Neck Circles
That snap, crackle, and pop you hear when rolling your neck is not breakfast cereal, it's bone rubbing on bone. This can wear down the bone and lead to degenerative changes in the vertebrae.

Safer Alternatives:

Move head forward and back, tilt head side to side, twist head side to side.

Toe Touches or Any Straight Leg Bending Against Gravity
This places a great deal of unnecessary strain on the lower back. One wrong move and you can easily throw your back out.

Sitting down while performing this activity eliminates the strains of gravity and reduces the possibility of back injury.

Bending and Twisting, While Lifting
Improper lifting puts severe strain on the vertebral disks, muscles, and ligaments of the lower back. Never use your back to lift, unless you enjoy hospital food.

Bring the object you are lifting directly in front of your feet. Bend your knees, keep your head up and back straight. Bring the object in close and lift with your legs, not your back.

Improper Sit-Ups or Leg-Lifts
If the pelvis is not kept flat on the ground (no arch in the lower back) while doing sit-ups, you will over-strengthen the hip flexor muscles which can lead to a pelvis tilted downward in the front, low back pain, and pain down the back of the leg. Leg lifts also over-strengthen the hip flexor muscles if the lower back rises off the ground.

Sit-ups: Squeezing the large seat muscles together during this entire exercise will move your pelvis backwards and help you strengthen the proper muscles (the rectus abdominis).
One-Leg Leg-Lifts: Always keep the lower back touching the ground and one knee bent, foot flat, and do leg lifts with the straight opposite leg. Reverse.
Curl-ups: Lying on your back, knees bent, feet flat, low back flat, keep your pelvis rotated backward and sit up about 6 to 8 inches only. Hold for a two count and then lower slowly. Repeat.

Pulling Heavy Objects Towards You
This can strain the back and throw your spinal column out of alignment.

The human body is more suited to pushing objects than pulling them. Use your strong seat muscles, thighs, and calves, not your tiny, weak back muscles to do the work.

Bounce Stretching (Ballistic Stretching)
Avoid this type of exercise if you can. It's too easy to go past the limits of your joints resulting in pain and injury.

Don't try to force your muscles to stretch abruptly; it's much safer and effective to perform slow, relaxed, smooth, steady stretches. Let them relax and lengthen during stretching.

Activities to Avoid, or Use with Caution:

Holding the Breath While Exercising
You may pass out or elevate your blood pressure to dangerous levels.

Isometric Exercises
Avoid these exercises if you're over 35 years of age. Isometrics can raise your diastolic blood pressure to dangerous levels, cutting off oxygen to your brain and heart.

Very Deep Squats
These exercises can damage the internal structures of your knee joints, leading to chronic pain and inflammation.

Running with Improper Footwear
Shoes not suited for running can lead to flat feet, achilles tendonitis, shin splints, and knee or back pain.

Back Raises with Weights
These exercises consist of hanging your upper body over a bench, face down, and raising up with a weight behind your head. Back raises can damage the vertebrae of your lower back and strain your lower back muscles.

Hip Inward Rotation and Adduction
Rotating the hip inwards, while simultaneously bringing the leg across to the other side, has a tendency to pull the head of the femur (thigh bone) out of the socket.

Safer Alternatives:

Always breathe normally during exercise, particularly when doing heavy exertion.

Build muscular strength and endurance by lifting light weights through the whole range of joint motion.

Don't squat deeper than a 90° angle between upper and lower legs. Don't squat with heavy weights. Perform knee straightening and bending with ankle weights or on a weight machine. Swim with fins.

Use shoes that absorb shock, have good arch support, and prevent ankle turning. It also helps to run on soft surfaces and to stretch before and after running.

Lie on your abdomen with hands by your shoulders; push up, extending arms half way, while keeping abdomen on the mat.

Lie on your back, put the soles of your feet together, bring your heels to your seat bottom, and let gravity pull your knees towards the floor (hold for 60 seconds).

EXERCISE RECOMMENDATIONS

Problems associated with stress frequently come from the lack of proper exercise. Improper posture, shortened muscles, headaches, pain, poor circulation and balance, decreased endurance and strength, and finally, a poor self-image are all too common hallmarks of a sedentary life. To maintain health and reduce stress, you should routinely practice cardio-respiratory (aerobic) endurance exercises. Aerobic exercises develop the heart and lungs by keeping your large muscle groups moving continuously over a prolonged period of time. Brisk walking, hiking, bike-riding, swimming, cross-country skiing, dancing, and jogging are some of the best aerobic endurance exercises. Golf, weight lifting, watching TV, calesthenics, and other start-and-stop activities do not help train the heart and lungs because the necessary intensity of exercise is not maintained for a long enough time.

Before embarking on an aerobics program, have a stress test done by an exercise physiologist or cardiologist. A stress test is vital because many heart problems are undetectable when you're at rest. The test will determine if any irregularities exist by checking how efficiently your heart uses and transports oxygen to your body during different levels of work.

The results of a stress test are then used to determine your training heart rate which tells you the intensity of exercise needed for improving aerobic endurance (training the heart) without killing yourself. If you don't want to go through the stress test, the following formula determines your training heart rate and the resulting range in which, barring physical problems, you can safely improve your cardio-respiratory endurance.

Calculating a Training Heart Rate

Example: A 60-year-old person with a pulse (or resting heart rate) of 75. To determine your pulse or resting heart rate, take your fingertips (not thumbs) and feel just on the outside of the large tendon on the wrist beneath the thumb. Count the number of beats in ten seconds and then multiple by six:

	Example	Your Chart
Maximum Heart Rate	220	220
Subtract Your Age	−60	− *28*
	160	___
Subtract Pulse	−75	− *51*
Heart Rate	= 85	*111*

Multiply Heart Rate   85   85   85   *111*   ___   ___

by 60%, 70%, 80%   x .60   x .70   x .80   x .60   x .70   x .80

= 51   = 59.5   = 68   = *66.6*   = *77.7*   = *88.8*

Add Your Pulse: + 75   + 75.0   + 75   + *51*   + *51*   + *51*

This is the range for your training heart rate:

(Beats per Minute) = 126   =134.5   = 143   = *147.6*   = *158.7*   = *169.8*

The three numbers of your training heart rate are now your guides to aerobic exercise. To improve aerobic endurance, you need to exercise vigorously enough to bring your pulse up to your Training Heart Rate range (in the above case, 126-143 beats per minute) and then maintain that intensity for at least 20 minutes, three to four times per week. Exercising at a lesser intensity for a shorter time or fewer days, reduces the training effect and may eliminate it altogether.

Ultimately, aerobic training is essential for reducing stress and improving health and longevity. Of course, don't run right out and try to increase your pulse instantly. Start slowly and gradually increase your efforts. If you feel pain, especially in your chest, slow down or stop. Be prepared for a few sore spots in muscles that haven't been exercised recently. However, after getting over the first few days of new exercises you'll see a rapid and marked improvement in yourself. If you stick with it and train routinely, these exercises will help to lower your blood pressure and pulse, improve your ability to use oxygen during exertion, increase the efficiency of your heart and lungs, and burn off excess muscle tension and lots of calories.

AEROBIC TRAINING TIPS

Have a stress test done or determine your own target heart rate.

Record your pulse (resting heart rate).

Select aerobic activities you enjoy.

Start slow and build up gradually. (You didn't get out of shape in one day and, therefore, it will take more than one day to get back in shape.)

Wear comfortable shoes that have good shock absorption, arch support, and resist ankle turning.

Always warm up before exercising. Gently move your joints through their normal range of motion 8 to 10 times to prepare yourself for action (range of motion is described later on). Then after warming up stretch out four tight muscles.

Always cool down after exercising. Don't sit down immediately after concluding a workout; keep moving until your heart rate slows to near your resting pulse rate. If you stop moving immediately after exercising, your blood may pool in your feet, creating the possibility of a blackout. By continuing movement during cool down, your muscles act as pumps that squeeze blood back to the heart, reducing its burden.

Stretch after cooling down.

Frequently monitor your pulse to be sure you are maintaining the proper intensity of exercise for the appropriate length of time. A wrist stopwatch or a jogging watch is very handy.

Exercise at 60 to 80% of your target heart rate for 20 to 50 minutes, 3 to 4 times a week.

Get into an enjoyable routine by yourself, with friends, or in a class, and then don't deviate from it.

AHH, JUST A LITTLE MORE!

CHAPTER 6: POSTURE AND STRESS

Posture, or body alignment, refers to the overall balance of your body and its parts. Good posture protects your body from injuries and deformities. Stress, poor posture, and lack of proper exercise can alter your body's normal balance and lead to pain, headaches, decreased flexibility, skeletal changes, and chronic fatigue. If you have poor posture, postural re-alignment exercises are an important part of your personal stress reduction plan. Look at Section 2 of your Personal Stress Inventory to determine the exercises that you need.

PROPER AND IMPROPER POSTURE

How can you tell if you have good posture? Here's one easy way to check your front to back posture. Tie a weight on the end of a long string. Standing in your normal position, have someone hold the free end of the string level with the top of your head so the weight is just off the ground. If you have normal posture the string will pass midway between the heel and the ball of the foot, behind the knee cap, directly over the hip joint, then past the tip of the shoulder, and in line with the ear lobe.

Also, have the friend look at you from the front and back. If you have normal posture your friend will see an erect head with no side-to-side tilting, level shoulders, level shoulder blades (scapulae), level hips, no "C" or "S" curve of the spine, and no noticeable twists in the rib cage.

Normal Posture

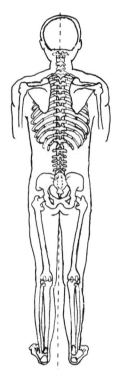

Side View   Back View

In most instances, poor posture is caused by muscular imbalances, that is, one group of muscles is stronger than its opposing group, and pulls the body out of balance. If these muscles are not re-balanced through exercise, the skeletal system will be permanently altered, causing pain and deformity. Poor posture is very common. Many people unconsciously succumb to poor postural habits, feeling that their deviated positions are correct.

Poor posture can be corrected by breaking the bad habits that caused the problem in the first place. The first step is recognizing when you are assuming poor posture and making a conscious effort to correct it. Then, practicing a series of realignment exercises will help to reverse the damaging affects of poor posture.

A Quick Guide to Posture Improvement

Carefully evaluate your posture. Compare it to the illustrations of proper posture. Pinpoint those parts of your body that need work.

Select exercises (from those described in the next pages) recommended for reducing your postural faults. Practice the exercises routinely.

Make a conscious effort to be more aware of your posture and keep it correct.

Check your posture frequently in a mirror or by having a friend look for improper posture symptoms.

When you feel pains in the neck, shoulders, back, or have a headache, check your posture, correct it, and relax all tight muscles.

If you sit or drive a great deal, get a good chair or a back support cushion to prevent you from slouching.

Sleep on a good mattress.

Remember how your mother used to poke you in the back and say: "Sit up straight or you'll become a hunchback." Take her advice.

COMMON POSTURE FAULTS AND
RECOMMENDED REALIGNMENT EXERCISES

The following exercises will help restore your body alignment to its normal balance and equilibrium. All of the exercises are beneficial, but be sure to try those that correct the posture problems you identified on your PSI. Make the appropriate exercises a permanent part of your personal stress reduction plan.

Problem: Forward Head.

The head and neck are carried too far forward (the ear lobe is in front of the vertical gravity line). This condition produces muscle tension, degenerative joint problems, pain in the muscles of the back of the neck, and headaches.

A forward head comes from tight muscles on the front of the neck and weak muscles of the upper back just below the neck.

Exercises for a Forward Head:

Neck Realignment. Bring your chin to your chest. Then, while maintaining a chin down position, use the muscles of your upper back to gently bring your head erect back into proper alignment. Do not force this exercise. Do not raise your chin up in the air because this will be strengthening the wrong muscles. Breathing slowly and deeply, let your shoulder muscles relax and hold your head in its proper posture for about 20 seconds. Develop a feel for this position and try to maintain it, particularly when getting a headache, stiff neck, or pains in the neck.

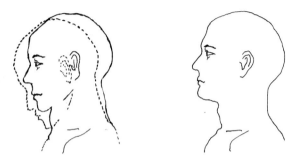

Wall Neck Exercise. Place your back to a wall, bend your knees slightly, flatten your lower back, bring your shoulders back and then bring your chin down and head back. Try to gently bring the back of your neck to the wall. Breathe slowly and deeply, holding for 20 seconds.

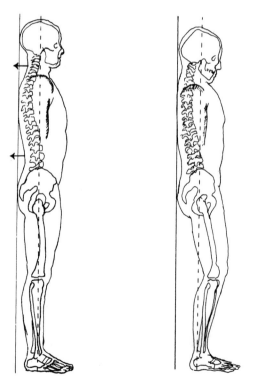

Some Other Remedies for a Forward Head

Special neck pillows (see Chapter 8) and cervical traction pillows (see Chapter 9) can significantly help reduce problems caused forward head.

If you have severe neck and shoulder pain that radiates down your arm, see a doctor; particularly a musculo-skeletal specialist who will do something other than prescribe drugs that simply cover up the symptoms. A good specialist, such as a physical therapist, osteopath, or a chiropractor, can determine the exact problem and relieve it at its source. For instance, sometimes an out of alignment cervical vertebrae causes radiating pain that can be relieved by a simple skeletal adjustment. Why be in pain? See a doctor.

Additional Neck Exercises

Remember that neck circles can damage your spine. Here are other, safer neck exercises:

Head Tilt. While standing, tilt your head to the side (ear towards shoulder) and hold for 20 seconds. Don't force it, let gravity gently stretch out the muscles. Reverse.

Head Turning. While standing, rotate your head as far as possible to one side and hold for 20 seconds. Reverse. (Extra credit if you can go completely around -- just kidding!)

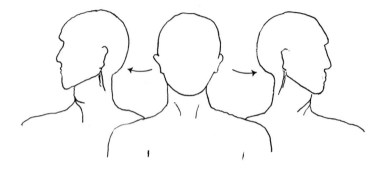

Prone Head Turning. While lying face down on a mat or rug, turn your head to one side, touching your ear to the mat. Hold for 20 to 60 seconds. Reverse.

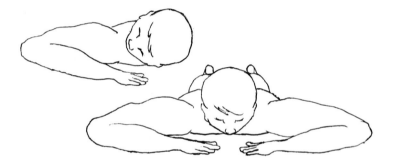

Superman's Stretch. Face down on a mat or rug, resting on your forehead and nose, stretch your arms above your head. Hold for 20 to 60 seconds.

Problem: Round Shoulders.

If your shoulders slope inwards so the tips fall in front of the vertical gravity line, you may experience pain in the shoulders and between the shoulder blades (scapulae). In severe cases you may have limited shoulder flexibility and difficulty breathing.

Round shoulders are usually caused by tight muscles on the front of the chest and shoulder (pectoralis minor and major, anterior deltoid and intercostal muscles) out of balance with weak muscles on the back between the shoulder blades (the rhomboids and middle and lower trapezius.

Exercises To Reduce Round Shoulders

Blade Squeeze. Clasp the hands behind the back, squeeze the shoulder blades together while raising the arms gently up in the rear. Hold for 20 seconds. Squeeze the buttocks (gluteals) together while doing this exercise to prevent bending forward at the trunk.

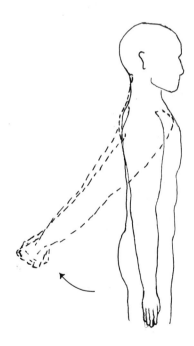

Shoulder Rolls. While slowly breathing in, smoothly and slowly raise the shoulders. When they are completely elevated, squeeze the shoulder blades together. Then, exhale as slowly as possible while slowly lowering the shoulders. Repeat up to three times.

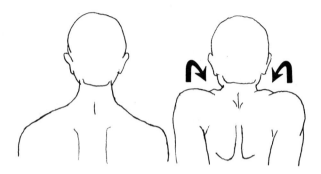

Back Forearm Grasp. With the arms behind the back, grasp the opposite forearm with one hand and squeeze the shoulder blades together. Hold for 20 seconds. Reverse.

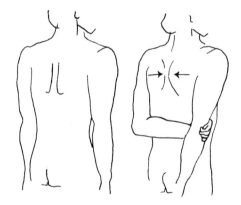

Up and Under. Try to join the hands together behind the back with one arm coming down from your head and the other arm reaching up from your waist. Hold for 20 seconds. Reverse.

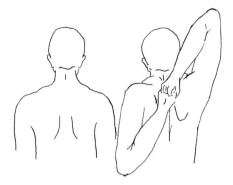

Shoulder Stretcher. With fingers interlaced behind the head or the hands on the shoulders with the fingers touching the neck, squeeze the shoulder blades together in the rear. Hold for 20 seconds. Relax. Repeat.

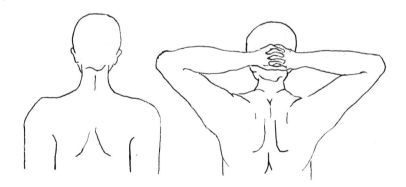

Airplane. Lying on your abdomen, put your arms to the sides like airplane wings and then raise the shoulders off the ground by squeezing the shoulder blades together. Relax. Repeat.

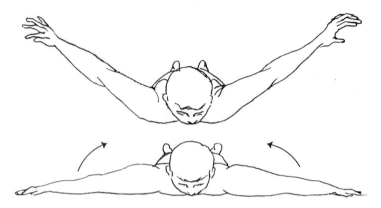

Additional Exercises for Round Shoulders

Bar Hang. Hold on to a high bar with both hands and hang from it for as long as possible to stretch tight chest and shoulder muscles.

Wing Stretches. Put fists together in front of chest, squeeze the shoulder blades together for a few seconds and then return to starting position. Repeat 10 to 20 times.

Jolsons Stretch. With arms straight out to the sides, take a step forward with one leg (bending the knee of the front leg) while squeezing the shoulder blades together. Repeat 10 times. Reverse.

Hand Clap. Clap hands in front and then in back 10 times. Clap behind back and above head 10 times.

Stretch in a Doorway. Hold each side of a doorway, about shoulder high or higher. Let your head and torso fall through the open doorway while your hands support you. Feel the stretch in your chest. Vary the height of your hands to stretch different muscles. Hold for 20 seconds.

The Wallneck Exercise (described earlier) also combats round shoulders.

Problem: Low Back Misalignment.

A pelvis that is tilted forward (lower in the front of the body) may interfere with nerve routes running out of the spine causing pain, muscle spasms, a disc herniation, or a ruptured disc. Low back pain is one of the most common ailments.

Back misalignment is frequently caused by a combination of weak abdominal and seat (gluteal) muscles out of balance with tight hip flexor and low back (lumbar extensors) muscles. In normal posture these two groups of muscles counteract each other like a seesaw.

Muscles Influencing Pelvic Alignment

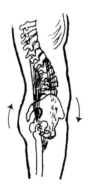   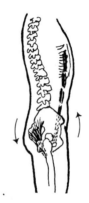

Hip Flexor and Lumbar Extensor Action   Abdominal and Gluteal Action

The figures above illustrate the bowstring principle. The hip flexors and lumbar extensors pull the pelvis forward and tilt it causing an increased arch in the low back, while the gluteals and abdominals act in an opposite manner pulling the pelvis backwards. If the hip flexors and lumbar extensors are too tight and the abdominals and gluteals are too weak, the pelvis tilts to the front producing a misaligned lower back.

You can correct this type of pelvic tilt by stretching out the hip flexors and lumbar extensors and then strengthening the abdominals and gluteals. When exercising to realign the pelvis, a good rule to follow is stretch before you strengthen and then stretch again.

53

Exercises to Stretch the Hip Flexors

Hip Flexor Stretch. Lying on your back, bring one knee to the chest while keeping the other leg straight and completely in contact with the floor. The arrow indicates where you should feel muscles stretching. Hold for 60 seconds. Reverse.

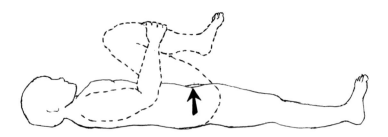

Hip Flexor Stretch (hands and knees). Start on your hands and knees. Lift one knee up and put the foot flat in between both hands. Slide the other knee back as far as possible. Now, with your head up bring your hips as far forward as possible. The arrow indicates where you should feel muscles stretching. Hold for 30 to 60 seconds. Reverse. During this exercise your front leg's calf muscles are also being stretched.

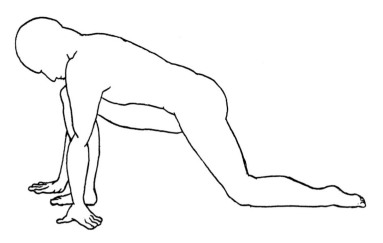

Exercises to Stretch the Low Back

<u>Low Back (lumbar extensor) Stretch</u>. Lying on your back, bring both knees to your chest and hold for 60 seconds.

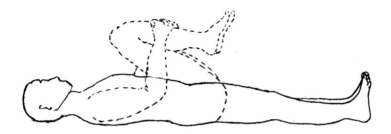

<u>Rollers on Back</u>. Bring both knees to your chest and gently roll forward and back, and then side to side. Repeat ten times each way.

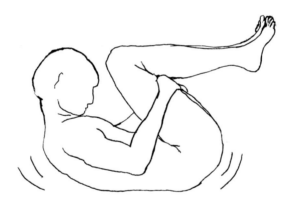

Low Back Stretch While Seated. While seated with your legs directly in front of you, bend forward slowly, allowing gravity to gently stretch your low back and hamstring muscles. Hold for 30 to 60 seconds. Do not force the muscles. If you feel pain, stop immediately.

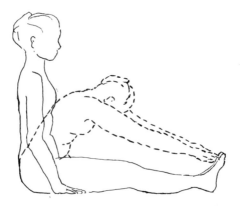

Moslem Prayer Position. Get on all fours and then sit backwards on your heels. Bend forward and place your arms comfortably above your head. This position gently stretches the lower back. Hold for 30 to 60 seconds.

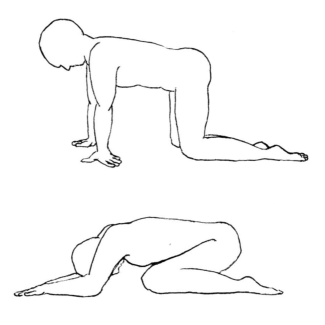

Exercises to Strengthen the Abdominals

Modified Sit-up. Lying on your back, bend your knees and lock your fingers behind your neck. Sit up and touch opposite elbow to knee. Move the knee so it meets the elbow halfway in the sit-up. Return to starting position. Alternate sides. Keep your head back so you use only the abdominals and not the neck muscles. As you feel better about this exercise, reach further with the elbows and less with the knees. Repeat until fatigued. Don't hold your breath.

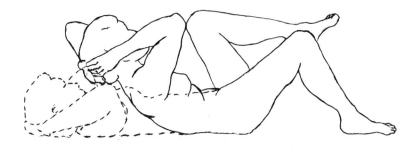

Abdominal Curl. Lie on your back, with knees bent and feet flat on the floor. Keeping your chin tucked to your chest and low back flat, curl up off the mat (using only the abdominals) for the count of "one thousand one, one thousand two". Return to the starting position. Repeat until fatigued. Do not use the neck muscles. It's not important to raise up to the knees, just raise up unt'' the abdo. nals tighten.

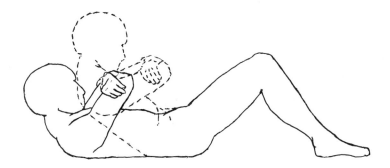

57

Elevated Knee Sit-Ups. Lie on your back and raise knees up to create a right angle between knees and lower legs. With hands behind head, neck relaxed, curl up using the abdominals. Repeat until fatigued.

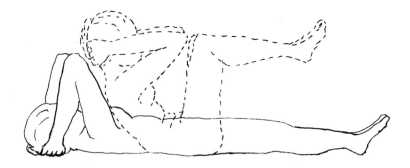

Triple Abdominal Strengthener. This is a three-part exercise that builds upon the first part. Avoid this activity if you have high blood pressure. Lying on back, knees bent, feet flat on the floor:

Suck in your abdomen and hold it in for 10 seconds, then continue to hold in the gut while simultaneously rotating your pelvis backwards to flatten your low back to mat. Hold for 10 seconds. While maintaining this position pull the lower ribs in. Hold for 10 seconds. Don't forget to keep breathing throughout this entire exercise. Relax. Repeat.

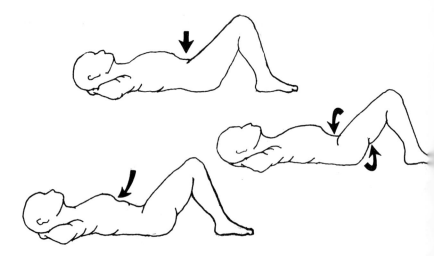

Exercises to Strengthen the Seat Muscles (Gluteals)

Pelvic Tilts. Lie on your back with knees bent, and feet flat on the floor. Contract your seat muscles and lower abdominal muscles. Holding these muscles firm, push your pelvis down until your lower back comes into direct contact with the floor. Relax. Repeat to tolerance.

Hip Tilts. Starting in the same position as for the Pelvic Tilts, squeeze the gluteals together to raise your hips off the floor. Relax. Repeat to tolerance.

Hip Hyperextension. Lying either on your abdomen or on all fours, raise a leg up in the rear, keeping it straight, and then lower it slowly. Do not arch your back. Try to tighten only the gluteals. Relax. Repeat to tolerance.

Supplemental Back Care Tips

Swimming is an excellent alternative exercise. Running can sometimes aggravate back injuries. '

Bicycle riding with high handlebars is also excellent.

You can sit more comfortably and relieve back strain by using specially designed back cushions that provide vital support to the proper points along your spine (see Chapter 9).

When standing for long periods, or when bending over a table, bed, or sink, place one foot on a foot stool to keep pressure off your lower back. (This long-recognized means for relieving back stress is why saloons have a railing around the base of their bars.)

Trunk Rotation Exercises

Trunk Twisting. Standing with feet straight ahead, arms extended out in front, gently twist upper trunk and arms as far as possible to one side. Focus attention on hands. Hold. Reverse.

Spinal Twist. Sitting on a mat, place left leg over straight right leg with left foot perpendicular to right leg. Twist upper torso to the left, placing both hands on your left side. Hold. Reverse.

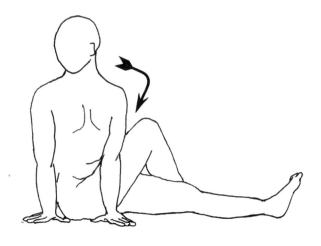

ADDITIONAL SAFE EXERCISES

Problem: Poor Shoulder Flexibility

Shoulder Internal and External Rotation. Hold one arm out horizontally. Bend your elbow to 90°. Point fingers to the floor and then to the ceiling, without moving the upper arm out of its horizontal position. Point up and down 10 times. Relax. Repeat with other arm.

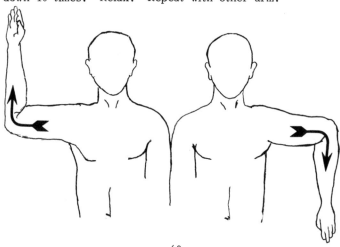

Shoulder Circles. With *palms up* and arms held straight out horizontally, rotate at the shoulder in 5 to 10 small circles, 5 to 10 medium circles, and then 5 to 10 large full circles. Reverse directions and repeat.

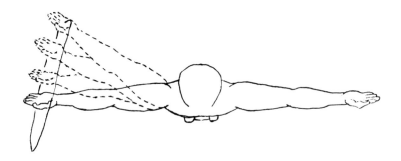

Shoulder Flexion. With arms in front of you, interlock fingers, palms down. Raise straight arms up, stretching above head, pushing palms towards ceiling, Hold for 5 to 10 seconds. Relax. Repeat.

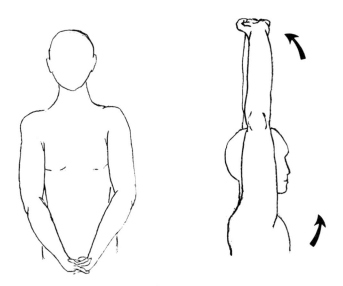

Shoulder Shrugs. Raise each shoulder up and down 10 times.

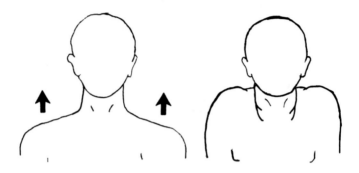

Overhead Arm Raise. Both arms by sides, head bent forward, slowly inhale and raise head up and arms out to the sides until hands meet above your head. Stop inhaling when your hands reach their peak height. Exhale and slowly reverse. Repeat.

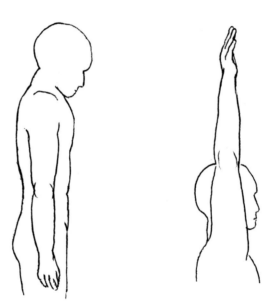

Problem: Poor Hip Flexibility

Exercises to Improve Hip Flexibility

Hip External Rotation. Lie on your back, hands behind head, knees bent with soles of your feet together. Bring your heels close to your seat and then let gravity gently pull your knees sideways to the ground. Hold for 60 seconds. This exercise stretches the muscles on the inside of the thighs and helps to maintain a good solid hip socket.

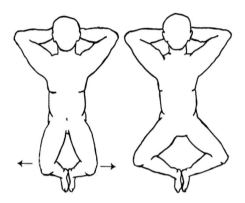

Side Knees. Lie on your back, knees slightly bent, with feet flat on the floor. Allow both knees to gently fall to the same side. Hold for 60 seconds. Reverse.

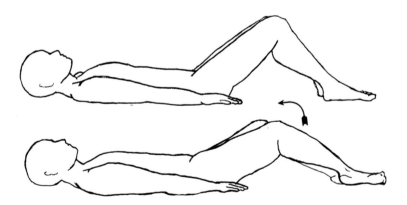

Problem: Tight Hamstring Muscles

Exercises to Stretch Hamstring Muscles

Seated Hamstring Stretch.   While sitting on the floor, keep one leg straight and place the sole of the other foot next to the thigh of the straight leg.   Take a deep breath while raising your arms above your head.   Exhale slowly and lean forward towards the straight leg.   Don't strain.   Hold for 30 to 60 seconds.   Reverse.

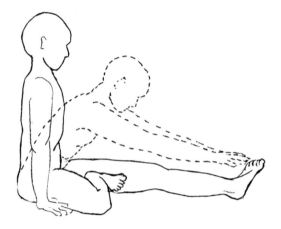

Standing Hamstring Stretch #1.   Place heel on chair, table, or a stair of appropriate height to stretch hamstring slowly.   Hold for 30 to 60 seconds.

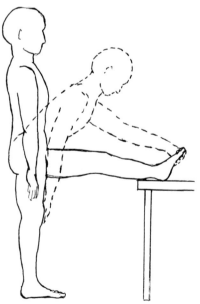

64

Standing Hamstring Stretch #2. Left foot straight ahead, right to the side (heels in line) about shoulder width apart, bend the left knee, turn the hips to the right and lean towards the straight right foot. It is important to keep the *rear knee bent* to avoid strain to the back. Reverse.

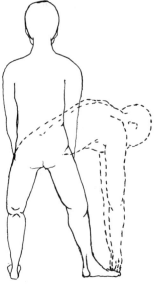

Hamstring and Calf Stretch. Lie on your back, with one knee bent, foot flat on the floor, and the other leg straight with its toe pointed. Raise the straight leg as far as possible and then bring the toes toward you. Hold. Reverse. If you feel no stretch, straighten the other leg and keep it flat on the ground. To stretch the muscles even more, put a belt or towel around the foot of the straight leg and pull on it while raising the leg.

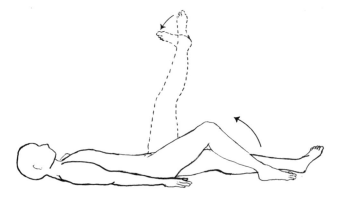

Problem: Tight Thigh Muscles

Exercises to Stretch Thigh Muscles

Quadricep Stretch. Sitting on your feet, lean backwards with arms behind to support your weight. Don't arch your lower back. Use this exercise with caution if you have knee problems.

Foot Grabber. Lie on your abdomen and bend one leg at the knee. Reach back and grab the foot and try to touch its heel to your seat. Hold. Reverse.

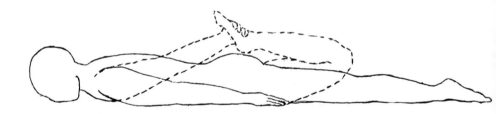

66

Lunges. Stand with your left foot forward and right to the side (heels in line). Bend your right knee and lunge towards the right. Repeat to tolerance. Reverse. Or, do this exercise by holding the stretched position for 20 seconds. Increase time as tolerance increases.

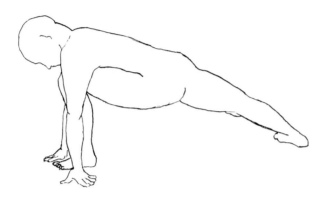

Problem: Tight Calf Muscles

Exercises to Stretch Calf Muscles

Calf Stretcher. Place fully extended arms against a wall with one foot forward, knee slightly bent, and the other foot back, leg straight, toes slightly inward. Keep the rear heel flat on the floor. The further back the rear heel is the greater the calf stretch. Hold for 60 seconds. Reverse.

Soleus Stretch. Assume same position as the Calf Stretcher, but bring your rear heel half the distance closer to the front foot. Bend both knees until you feel the stretch and hold the position for 30 seconds. Reverse.

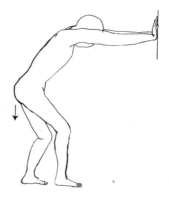

Stair Calf Stretch. Stand on the lowest stair of a staircase. Hold on to the banister and hang the back half of one foot over the stair's edge. Keep your toes or forefoot on the stair while gradually lowering your heel. You'll feel the calf stretch as the heel goes lower than the toes. Hold for 30 seconds. Reverse. You can also do both feet at the same time. Be careful not to slip off the stair.

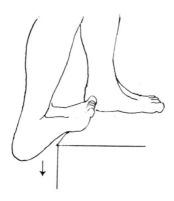

Getting Your Exercise Program Going

Now that you know the exercises for realigning your posture and reducing stress, it's time to get a solid, safe program going. Whether you've already begun a posture exercise program and are practicing it twenty minutes, three times a week or are starting out completely new, the first requirement is the same: a weekly routine that you firmly maintain. Each week, schedule at least three posture exercise periods lasting a minimum of 30 minutes. Try to find a quiet and peaceful environment for doing the exercises. A living room or family room works well.

If you're already in an aerobics program, you can combine the two exercise programs or, alternatively, simply do the posture exercises on the day you don't do aerobics. Once you've established your exercise time, try to stick to it, until it becomes a familiar routine. Initially, "finding the time for exercising" may be difficult but, after getting into a routine you may be surprised at how eagerly you look forward to the exercises, how good they make you feel, and how easily they fit into your busy schedule.

Here's the basic routine that works for posture realignment exercises: Warm up each joint by slowly moving it through its normal range of motion five to ten times. Start at the neck and work down the body, moving every joint including the finger and toes. Try to get comfortable in each exercise position. Relax your mind and body and maintain proper breathing during all stretching and realignment exercises. Take long, slow, deep, complete, diaphragmatic breaths and bring calmness to your mind and body. Never strain. Let your muscles lengthen and relax more each time you inhale and exhale.

CHAPTER 7: DEEP RELAXATION:
THE ART OF DOING NOTHING

Long ago, people realized that the regular practice of deep relaxation produces important physiological, psychological and spiritual benefits. Many of the relaxation techniques developed by ancient cultures were often associated with religious lifestyles, such as Yoga and Zen. The ancient Hebrews and Egyptians also practiced deep relaxation, but to a lesser extent.

Our ancestors realized that setting aside some time each day to deeply rest their minds and bodies was essential for good health. Until recently, this practice was all but abandoned by our fast-paced society that traditionally sees relaxation as an unproductive waste of time.

Reading, watching television, and spectator sports are very popular forms of relaxation but, unfortunately, do not provide the deep relaxation necessary to combat stress. In fact, these forms of relaxation bombard the central nervous system with stimulation that actually adds to your stress level. Quality relaxation comes from the quiet times when you think your own peaceful thoughts, relax your tight muscles, calm your emotions, rest your mind, and do absolutely nothing.

There are many ways to deeply relax; some people take cat naps, some sit quietly and reflect upon their own thoughts, while others practice focused breathing or transcendental meditation. As long as the technique is natural and doesn't involve drugs, routinely practicing deep relaxation effectively reverses the negative effects of stress. Which techniques is best for you? You won't know until you try a variety and find the deep relaxation method optimum for your body, mind, and state of stress. Then, after you've found the one for you, making it part of your comprehensive stress reduction plan will improve your health immensely.

RELAXATION TIPS

Begin with the proper attitude. Have an open mind and no anxiety about your possible success or failure. *Everyone* succeeds because relaxation is simply doing nothing. To succeed all you have to do is passively will relaxation to occur. This "can't fail" attitude is one of the most important elements for learning how to relax.

Create the proper environment. A quiet, softly lit, comfortable place with a moderate temperature is the best place for relaxing. Disconnect the phone and hang up a "do not disturb" sign. A mat or a comfortable chair and soothing music or a prepared relaxation tape are also helpful. This is your special place to do nothing.

Stick to a routine. Reduced stress and improved health comes when you to practice 15-20 minutes of deep relaxation at least three times a week. Find a convenient time and set it aside for the sole purpose of deep relaxation. Some possibilities are before you go to work, coffee breaks, between classes, lunch time, or just after work. If your office isn't suitable, try lying or sitting in your car while listening to a prepared tape.

Expect to relax. Everyone experiences relaxation in his or her own special way. Some people explain the sensation as a tingling, followed by numbness and a sense of well being; others experience warmth, heaviness, and peacefulness. Don't try to steer and rationalize your experience, expect relaxation to happen and then just passively let it happen and enjoy.

RELAXATION TECHNIQUES

Focused Breathing.

As described in Chapter 4, controlled breathing is the key to relaxation. Begin each relaxation session with some long, slow, deep, diaphragmatic breaths, while focusing your entire awareness on the breathing process. Deep relaxation naturally occurs with focused breathing. If you've forgotten them, refer back to the breathing exercises in Chapter 4.

Muscular Relaxation.

Are your muscles tight? Can you tell when they're relaxed? Here are some muscle relaxation techniques to help you recognize and relax tight muscles. The techniques also burn off excess muscle tension, increase your body awareness, and ultimately, help you deeply relax.

Contract-Relax - Contract one muscle, or a group of muscles for five seconds (don't hold your breath) and then relax the muscle by doing the opposite of contracting it--doing nothing. For best results, exercise every muscle or muscle group in the body this way. Work from head to toe or toe to head.

Contract-Relax with Resistance - Contract a muscle or muscle group while pushing or pulling against an immovable object. For instance, when contracting the muscles in the back of your upper arm (the triceps muscle) push down on a desk top with your fingertips at the same time. This resistance technique forces greater muscular contractions which increases your ability to feel the difference between the contracted and relaxed state. As before: don't hold your breath while doing this exercise.

Diminishing Tensions - After contracting a muscle (with or without the extra resistance), slowly and incrementally relax it bit-by-bit by counting backwards from 5. Thus, you contract a muscle for 5 seconds -- 1-2-3-4-5, and then relax it a little bit more on each number, 5-4-3-2-1. At the one, the muscle is completely relaxed.

Biofeedback - The use of an electromyograph or electromyometer provides you with a reading (in microvolts) of a muscle's actual tension. Biofeedback training teaches you to will muscles to relax by letting you see how the microvolt readout changes in response to your thoughts and stresses. (See Chapter 9 for more information about biofeedback.)

Autogenic Training.

This relaxation technique effectively reduces blood pressure, improves circulation to the hands and feet, promotes an overall feeling of deep relaxation, and relieves migraine headaches. Sit or lie down in your quiet relaxation place. Close your eyes and relax by focusing on your breathing or doing some of the muscular relaxation exercises. Then, silently and slowly repeat suggestions of warmth, heaviness, and deep relaxation to yourself. Don't try to force these suggestions to come true; just passively will them to occur. Silently repeat each phrase for up to 30 seconds.

Examples of self-relaxation phrases (substitute right and left, and hands, legs, and feet where appropriate):

My right arm and hand are growing warm and heavy.

My right hand is growing warmer and warmer.

Warmth is flowing into my hand(s).

My arms and hands feel heavy and warm.

My arms and hands feel warm, comfortable, and completely relaxed.

I feel quiet and warm.

I feel relaxed, comfortable, and peaceful.

My whole body is completely relaxed.

My chest and abdomen are completely relaxed.

I feel warm, heavy, and deeply relaxed.

My thoughts are calm and peaceful.

My whole body feels relaxed, comfortable, and peaceful.

My body feels limp and loose like a rag doll.

I feel like butter in a frying pan.

Visual Imagery (Day Dreaming).

Most people practice deep relaxation without even knowing it. Day dreaming is essentially a form of deeply relaxing meditation, although it's not as deep, controlled, or relaxing as a planned meditation experience. When you daydream, your eyes roll up into their sockets, pointing at a spot above and between the eyebrows. Your whole body relaxes, brain waves slow, and you see a mental picture from what is commonly called "the mind's eye," "third eye," or "mirror of the mind."

The slowing of the brain waves that occurs during a daydream is the key to relaxing. When you're aware, alert, and have all senses functioning, your brain wave rate will be thirteen cycles per second or above. This is known as the beta level of consciousness and is associated with being attentive, oriented and anxious. While daydreaming, the brain wave rate slows down to the alpha level, or between 8 and 13 cycles per second. Alpha brain waves represent a state of rest, relaxation, and relief from attention and concentration. The five senses are abandoned and the external world is "turned off."

In addition to providing deep physiological rest, the alpha state allows you to momentarily change your mental perspective. During daydreams you can clear your mind, and distance yourself from your thoughts. The result is an altered viewpoint that opens your mind to new thoughts and unleashes your full measure of creative intelligence. After twenty minutes in the alpha state, your brain will be far more efficient in carrying out its normal beta activities with increased clarity and renewed vigor. Consequently, the ability to reduce your brain wave rate to alpha at will, improves your ability to relax at will.

Here are some imagery examples that will improve your ability to voluntarily produce alpha brain wave rates and deeply relax. Read through the list and pick an image that seems pleasant for you. Then, make yourself comfortable in a quiet, isolated location, free from distractions. Close your eyes and practice some focused breathing and muscle relaxation exercises. While in a relaxed state, passively direct all of your energy to seeing the image you have selected. As you think about the image your brain will enter the alpha level of consciousness, just as if you were daydreaming. The images are:

In your mind picture your perfect place of relaxation. This is a place that you can mentally travel to whenever you are stressed. Think about mountains, waterfalls, tropical islands, the ocean, the desert, or whatever place relaxes you the most.

Picture fond childhood memories. Re-live a picnic with your parents, the holiday season with your family, your favorite birthday party, or your first bicycle.

Picture a field of beautiful flowers fluttering in the soft warm breeze. Notice the kinds and colors of flowers. Try to develop a sense of color in your mind's eye. Think about lying back in a hammock and letting the warm gentle breeze rock you into a deep state of relaxation.

Imagine you are floating on raft on a clear, warm ocean. The waves are gently rocking you underneath a blue sky dotted with large white puffy clouds. The sea air smells of salt and you can hear the gulls in the air as the relaxed pitch of the waves gently rocks you into a deep state of relaxation.

Picture yourself as a bird gliding on a warm breeze. See through the bird's eyes and watch the ground pass slowly beneath you. Notice what kind of bird you've become.

Picture white healing light surrounding you, your loved ones, or anyone who needs some positive energy. This light charges you with energy; you feel strong, confident, and deeply relaxed.

Let whatever thoughts that come into your mind flow freely. Just watch the pictures and let your imagination run wild.

Picture a pebble dropping into the still surface of a pond. Notice the concentric ripples, then watch them disappear as the surface turns into a mirror once again.

Picture your own mental TV set or movie screen on which you can view anything you desire. Ask your subconscious for answers to questions or problems that you have, and then watch the answers on the screen. This is also a good way to memorize material as you prepare for a test.

In your mind, create your perfect chair. When you sit in this chair all of your troubles leave, your health improves, and you instantly become deeply relaxed.

Picture the most tense part of your body. Picture the muscle fibers and watch them lengthen as they grow more and more relaxed. Feel all physical sensation leave this muscle as a wave of relaxation takes it over. Then, spread this sensation to the rest of your body.

Picture yourself floating through a rainbow of colors, each color adding to your relaxation, vitality, health, and self actualization. Picture yourself becoming the person you want to be.

Picture yourself piloting an old wooden sailboat that is heading out on the cool, blue, calm ocean. Envision the boat's billowing sails, the blue horizon, the golden sunshine, and white froth breaking across the bow. Listen to the sounds of the wooden hull and mast creaking and straining as you glide across the glistening surface. Relax to the songs of the gulls and the gentle tones of the far-off bells ringing their melodious messages. You are in total control of your destiny. Feel the euphoria, confidence, and peacefulness of this adventure.

Picture yourself walking down an ancient marble staircase as you listen to the faint sounds of a flutist playing in the distance. When you reach the bottom you find that you are in a beautiful courtyard full of artistic treasures. You are surrounded by bronze, gold and marble statues, and the fragrant smell of exotic flowers in bloom. It is dark and the only light comes from the dancing flames of many candles burning. You come to a beautiful pool full of very warm, but not too hot, water. You take off your robe and descend into the water and find a lounge chair made precisely for you. You lie back with your head comfortably out of the water. You take a deep breath, deeply relax, and enjoy the peaceful sounds of the flute.

If you have a medical problem picture the affected organ, body part, or system as being colored black. Then see it surrounded by white light until it returns to its natural healthy appearance.

Create your own relaxing visual experiences. Try to think of peaceful, harmonious, beautiful thoughts.

Visual Detachment.

You can achieve a relaxed state by steadily staring at an external object, while simultaneously suppressing any stray thoughts or feelings. Direct all your awareness at a stationary, neutral object. The object could even be a specific part of your body; for example:

Nasal Gaze - With your eyes only half open, steadily gaze at the tip of your nose. When your eyes tire, close them completely and clear your mind for a full minute.

Frontal Gaze - Direct your full attention to the space at the root of your nose between your eyes. When they tire, close your eyes completely and clear your mind for a full minute.

Body Part Meditation - Using deep relaxation techniques, reduce your brain waves to the alpha level and then focus your awareness on a body part, such as your hand. If your thoughts wander, immediately concentrate more strongly on the body part.

If visual detachment exercises sound like "contemplating your navel" that's because they are traditional beginning exercises for people learning meditation. Meditation has, unfortunately, gotten a lot of bad press. Too often associated with "alternative lifestyles", meditation has gained the unfair reputation of being slightly out of the mainstream and therefore suspect. As it happens, some highly-respected and widely-admired people draw their energy from meditation and deep relaxation. For instance, former president John F. Kennedy had developed the ability to will himself to sleep almost instantly and was able to grab a few minutes of refreshing rest between meetings. Whether he called it meditation, or some other name, this ability to "sleep on the run" is one characteristic of advanced meditation.

After becoming proficient in visual detachment, you'll be able to increase your meditation powers too. The next step after visual detachment is auditory detachment in which sounds, rather than sight, bring on a relaxed state. Using key words or sounds (called a mantra in meditation), you can will your body and mind to relax. Ultimately, the goal of meditation is to create a completely restful void in your mind, uncluttered by any sights or sounds. In this deeply restful state, your thoughts and internal dialogue are completely still and you become totally relaxed.

Auditory Detachment.

Auditory detachment for deep relaxation uses a mellifluous, easily recited word that is repeated over and over again, either silently or aloud. The word, or words, help you focus your concentration and awareness. A common key word is OM, composed of three sounds: A, U, M. To begin auditory detachment inhale deeply and slowly. Then in a low, steady, controlled voice, say "aah." Make the sound come from the back of your mouth. Hold the sound until one third of your air is gone. Then, without stopping, transform the "aah" into an "oh" sound produced at the front of your mouth, giving it a nasal character. Hold the "oh" sound for your second 1/3 of breath. Again without stopping, transform "oh" into the "mmm" sound. Press your lips together and make the sound loud enough to vibrate strongly through your head and chest. Hold the sound until your breath is finished. Inhale. After 10 to 20 seconds to get your breath back (depending on lung capacity and control), spend several seconds in silence. Repeat the sound seven times. Try to still your body and mind by thinking peaceful thoughts.

You can use other sounds besides OM. They can be either natural or imagined. When you hear a natural source of repetitive sound, such as a waterfall, the ocean, wind, or the humming of bees, simply listen and focus your awareness on the sound. You can also use artificial sound sources to relax.

Music profoundly relaxes many people; so do tape recordings of outdoor sounds such as a breeze blowing through pine boughs. Experiment with different types of music and various sound effects to determine those that soothe you the most. Classical music is the best for some, the flute for others, while other people prefer tapes of only outdoor sounds. Combining the auditory methods with other relaxation techniques can be especially effective. When you feel tense, relax by repeating your key word or listening to music, breathing diaphragmatically, slowing your brain to its alpha level of consciousness, and then trying a visual imagery exercise or letting your thoughts flow freely.

A SAMPLE RELAXATION SESSION

Begin with five minutes of focused breathing while softly playing your favorite relaxation tape. Then do 5 to 10 minutes of muscular relaxation, relaxing each part of your body starting at the top of the head and working down to the tips of the toes. Say words of warmth and heaviness while relaxing. For example:

Relax the muscles of your forehead and scalp. Let this deep relaxation flow down your face to your eyebrows and muscles of your eyes. Relax the muscles of your cheeks. Let this wave of relaxation spread down to your lips and tongue. Relax all the muscles of your jaw. Go deeper and deeper into this tranquil state of deep relaxation. Your arms and hands feel heavy and warm, ... and so on.

Relax your entire body in this manner.

When physically relaxed, do 5 to 10 minutes of visual imagery or detachment exercises.

At the end of the relaxation period, make some positive statement to yourself such as: "I am slowly coming out of this deeply relaxed healthy state. I will be feeling much better than before. My eyesight will be improved, my blood pressure reduced, and my heart rate decreased. I will be less tense and more alert. On the count of three I will open my eyes feeling much better than before." Count - one, two, three - and open your eyes.

CHAPTER 8: GETTING A GOOD NIGHT'S SLEEP

Good sleep is essential for successfully managing stress and maintaining your health. Unfortunately, many people have lost the ability to effortlessly fall and remain asleep. They go to bed, toss and turn, can't turn off their minds or get comfortable, worry that they will feel horrible at work the next day if sleep doesn't come soon, and then wake up prematurely. If you have problems sleeping, you're not alone. Between 15 to 25% of the population experiences more than just an occasional bout of sleeplessness and has chronic insomnia. This can lead to:

Poor performance on the job

Absenteeism

Poor health

Decreased creativity

Lack of motivation

Low energy

Decreased effectiveness and efficiency

Irritability and hostility

Impaired ability to communicate

Red eyes and yawning

Clouded thinking

If you aren't sleeping well now, it's time to find out what's causing the problem and to develop a plan of action to solve it. Because many factors influence sleep, there's no single magic cure-all that works for everyone.

Your own individual plan may involve changing your eating habits, visiting a doctor, changing jobs or living conditions, seeing a psychologist, changing your lifestyle, and trying a variety of natural sleep improvement programs.

One thing you should avoid, if at all possible, is the use of sleeping pills because they are addictive, dangerous, and actually prevent the deepest part of the sleep cycle from occurring. Sleeping pills just mask the symptoms of poor sleep without confronting the problem.

The first step in developing your "good sleep plan" is understanding what happens during sleep.

A GOOD NIGHT'S SLEEP IS ...

The average good night's sleep consists of four to five 90 to 100 minute cycles. Each cycle includes four distinct stages and a condition known as Rapid Eye Movement, or REM. During REM, one of the deepest parts of your sleep, your eyelids remain shut but your eyeballs move back and forth rapidly as if you were watching a fast-paced game of tennis. Throughout the night, during both REM and the non-REM stages of sleep, your body and brain undergo a variety of changes necessary for good health.

Insomniacs experience the same sleep stages and body changes, but they spend less time in the deeper stages of sleep and REM and they often have their cycles interrupted by periods of wakefulness. Look at this following table to get a good idea of what happens in each sleep stage.

SLEEP CYCLE STAGES

Stage of Sleep	Quality of Sleep	Body Responses	Mental Responses
On the verge of sleep	The borderline between sleep and wakefulness	Decreasing muscle tension and overall activity, slowed heart rate and pulse rate, lower temperature	Relaxation; awareness is low and the mind drifts
Stage I	Light sleep; easily awakened; if awakened, a person might deny having slept	Temperature, heart and pulse rates continue to decline; regular breathing; eyes roll slowly	Feels like floating, thoughts drift
Stage II	Light to moderate sleep; easy to awaken with moderate noise	Bodily functions continue to decrease; eyes and body are still; snoring is common; eyes will not see if opened	Memory and thought processes diminished some thoughts; a person may vaguely remember dreams if awakened
Stage III	Deep sleep; requires louder noises to awaken	All body processes drop further, occasional movements; greater secretion of growth hormones	Rarely able to remember thoughts or dreams
Stage IV	Deepest sleep; very hard to awaken	More decline of body processes; occasional movements, eyes quiet; sleep-walking and bed-wetting occur during this stage	Totally oblivious; poor recall if awakened in this stage
REM (Rapid Eye Movement)	Extremely difficult to awaken	Rapid eye movements; large muscles paralyzed; toes, fingers, and facial muscles twitch; erection; irregular pulse and breathing; increase in temperature, heart rate, blood pressure and metabolic rates	Dreaming occurs about 85% of the time in this stage; vivid dream recall; possibly unconsciously resolving conflicts

SLEEP QUALITY COMPARISON

	Normal Adult Sleeper	Insomniac	Insomniac on Sleeping Pills
Sleep Onset	10-15 Min.	45-50 Min.	45-50 Min.
Total Stage 3 Sleep	30 Min.	30 Min.	0 Min.
Total Stage 4 Sleep	20 Min.	10 Min.	0 Min.
Total REM Sleep	100 Min.	60 Min.	30 Min.

Now armed with the knowledge about the sleeping process, you can begin solving your sleep problems. Almost all sleep problems fall into one or more of the four categories:

1) Difficulty in initiating sleep

2) Falling asleep soundly but waking up after an hour or two and having trouble getting back to sleep

3) Waking up after 5 to 6 hours still tired but can't fall back to sleep

4) Don't feel rested after a full 6 to 8 hours of sleep

Do you see yourself in any of these categories? Most people have suffered each type of sleep problem at least once in their lives. That's not unusual. It's when the problems are chronic that you know you've got a serious sleep disorder.

Keeping a Sleep Log

To find out the causes of your poor sleep, keep a sleep log for a week or more to determine any patterns to the problems (for example, you don't sleep well every Sunday evening). In the log, keep track of:

What foods you ate for dinner and what time you ate.

How much alcohol you drank.

What you did for the last hour before retiring.

What medications or drugs you took.

How long it took you to fall asleep.

The time (or times) you awakened.

The thoughts that were keeping you up.

Any other information you know is harming your sleep.

Also make a list of factors that you suspect are responsible for your interrupted sleep. The lists below are some common factors, but your own list is what's important.

82

FACTORS THAT COMMONLY INTERRUPT SLEEP

Surroundings
Too much noise
Too warm or cold
Too much light
Uncomfortable bed and pillow
Covers are too restricting

Diet
Too much caffeine
A heavy meal close to bedtime
Eating the wrong foods
Drugs and medications
Too much alcohol

Body
Too much energy
Breathing difficulties
Muscle twitches or cramps
Not enough sex
Trying to go to sleep at different times each night
Lack of proper exercise

Mind
Can't turn off thoughts
Nightmares
Thinking about work problems
Anxiety that you cannot pinpoint
Thinking about important events

HOW TO EXPERIENCE A GOOD NIGHT'S SLEEP

Set the Mood for Sleep. Your quest for good sleep begins where it all starts, in the bedroom. The bedroom is a place to sleep, rest, and recreate; it is not a place to work, eat or worry. The ideal mood for a bedroom is comfort, security, and relaxation. The bedroom most conducive to sleep is quiet, dark, dust free and moderately cool, about 60-65°F.

Have a consistent bedtime. Retiring at about the same time each night programs your internal clock into a regular sleep pattern.

Relax your mind. Avoid intellectually stimulating activities, such as watching an interesting movie or reading a thought provoking book near your bedtime. Also, don't go to bed worrying about sleeping. Try to go to sleep with a clear, calm, self-confident mind. To help relax your mind, silently repeat suggestions such as: "I'm going to sleep deeply and soundly the whole night through; I will awaken in eight hours completely relaxed, refreshed and invigorated; I will sleep like a baby all night long."

Reduce noise and light.

Fix that leaky faucet or noisy drain pipe.

Get a non-ticking, noiseless clock.

Buy a set of quality ear plugs made of rubber or wax (not the cheap kind made for swimming). One type that works well is called the E-A-R plugs and can be ordered from Time and Space Enterprises, 650 North Bronson Lane, Hollywood, CA 90004.

Unplug your phone.

Listen to soft music or environmental sound tapes.

Purchase a sound generating sleep machine such as the "Sleep Coaxer" or the "Sleep Mate". These devices mask out disturbing sounds with peaceful outdoor sounds such as rain, wind, and the surf.

If your spouse's snoring is a problem, move to a separate room.

Install room-darkening shades and lined curtains.

Wear eye shades while sleeping.

Have a comfortable bed. Something as easy to remedy as uncomfortable bedding could be your sleep problem. Try out different types of mattresses, pillows, and covers until you find the right combination. You can try different mattresses in stores or in hotels when you travel. If you have a particularly good night's sleep in a hotel, be sure to get the name and model number of the mattress. Mattresses come in many sizes and degrees of firmness. There's no right or wrong; whatever is most comfortable is best for you. Generally however, look for a mattress that supports your entire body without too much pressure at your shoulders and hips. Here are some other suggestions:

Married insomniacs should have twin beds.

Waterbeds provide warmth and comfort, but not enough support if you have a back disorder. They may also affect your sleep if your spouse is a restless sleeper. All the tossing about can create waves that will surely wake you. Thoroughly try out a waterbed before buying one.

Overly firm mattresses help a bad back, but the right balance between comfort and firmness is strictly an individual preference.

Don't be shy when shopping for a mattress. Lie down, relax, and try it out before you make an expensive mistake.

Make sure the mattress doesn't contain material that aggravates any allergies.

A good pillow can be as important as a good mattress. If you frequently get up in the morning with a stiff neck, sore shoulders or numb hands, most likely the problem is your pillow. A pillow should be comfortable, non-allergenic, cool, light, and designed to follow the normal curves of your neck. A good pillow will help you sleep in proper postural alignment, which, by the way, keeps your airway wide open.

Recently, stores devoted solely to back care and good sleep have opened in a number of cities. One line that they carry is newly-designed pillows. Try the pillows until you find the one that fits your neck. An excellent variety is the EZ Sleeper available from Posture Support Manufacturing Company. See the back of the book for ordering information.

Natural Curve Neck Pillow

Finally, don't forget comfortable sheets and covers.

Try blue or green covers, sheets, and pajamas. They tend to have a sedating effect.

Have sheets that are cool, smooth and clean.

Leave enough room under the bed covers so your feet can move freely with no restrictions.

Use only the amount of blankets you need to keep warm.

Fall asleep in a good position. Sleeping on your abdomen is bad for your back. Try to fall asleep lying on your back or side with your head supported by a neck pillow. Keep your spine (neck included) in a straight line if possible. If you awake with one group of muscles consistently cramped or sore, concentrate on getting those muscles as comfortable as possible as you fall asleep.

Exercise more during the day. If you have a high energy level but a sedentary job, you may not be physically tired at bedtime. Exercising during the day, not right before bed, will help to tire you out. Participating in a regular routine of exercise such as brisk walking, swimming or cycling, and total body stretching will help you sleep better. See Chapters 5 and 6 for other aerobic and stretching exercises that will help you sleep better. You can even clean your house before going to bed. It's tiring, boring and gets you ready for a good night's rest.

Sex before sleep. Satisfying sex can help you sleep more deeply and happily. However, if you have problems with sexual performance, anxiety or impotence, sex at bedtime may hinder your sleep. Use your judgement.

Focused breathing and deep relaxation. Focused breathing and deep relaxation calm your mind, turn off that little voice inside you, deeply relax your body, and bring on the onset of sleep. Start your sleep time with long, slow deep breaths, muscle relaxation, visual and auditory detachment exercises, and silent, positive statements of how your sleep is going to be deep, restful, and healthy. (Refer to Chapters 4 and 7 for the breathing and deep relaxation techniques. You may also benefit from listening to a tape recording that induces relaxation and a deep natural state of sleep. See the back of this book for ordering instructions.)

Massage. Massaging all parts of your body produces an all-over feeling of relaxation that helps induce sleep, eliminate pain, and prevent muscle cramps. Chapter 9 tells how to massage yourself or someone else.

Warm Water. Warm water can relieve pain, reduce muscle spasms and tension, and produce an overall feeling of relaxation that can help you sleep. Take a warm bath, a shower with a shower massage, or sit in a jacuzzi before retiring for the evening. You can also give yourself a brief massage with the towel as you dry off.

Your Diet. Your diet may cause your sleeping problems. What you eat, when you eat, as well as how you eat can all be significant. Keep track of your eating habits in your sleep log and then see if your sleepless nights match a pattern in your eating behavior. For example, you may find that a glass of wine before bed that you thought helped you sleep actually is the cause of periods of wakefulness. Diet, like so much else related to stress, affects each person differently, but there are some general practices that help you sleep better:

Overeating, and the "stuffed" feeling that follows disturbs sleep. Eat a moderate evening meal.

Eat as early in the evening as possible.

Chew your food slowly and thoroughly.

Avoid evening meals that include heavy, spicy or greasy foods, or any foods that give you gas or indigestion.

Avoid foods that disagree with you or make you feel uncomfortable.

Avoid all caffeine (coffee, tea, and soft drinks).

Avoid foods with high amounts of sugar, salt, and starch. Particularly stay away from foods with artificial flavors and colors, and those considered junk food.

Check all the medications you are taking and avoid those that list insomnia as a side effect.

Limit alcohol intake; too much alcohol disrupts the normal sleep cycle.

Drink a glass of warm milk.

Don't eat when overtired.

Natural Sleep Improving Agents. Many natural products have a sedative and tranquilizing effect. Used in place of sleeping pills or other artificial drugs, the natural products can help you get a deep, relaxing sleep.

Tryptophan (500 mg) is a naturally occurring amino acid (in fact, one of the essential amino acids your body needs) that speeds the onset of sleep. For best results, take two of these safe, non-addicting tablets twenty minutes before bedtime. Tryptophan is available in drug and health food stores.

Calcium Complex (375 mg) and *Magnesium* (150 mg) combine to act as a natural muscle relaxant. One to four of these tablets taken daily with or after meals reduces muscle spasms and help you sleep.

B vitamin supplements of B3, B6, and B12 help combat insomnia. Recommended daily dosage: Niacinamide (B3) - 50 mg, (B6) - 50 mg, (B12) - 100 mg.

Potassium (98 mg) relieves muscle cramps. If you are deficient in potassium, you may frequently awaken with muscle cramps and/or twitches. Take one tablet a day or eat more bananas (an excellent source of potassium). Also try massage, muscle relaxation, and stretching the cramping muscles before bedtime.

Herbs have been used for centuries to help people sleep. The <u>Herb Book</u>, by John Lust, lists thirty-seven herbs or derivations from these plants to treat insomnia. Herb teas are some of the oldest concoctions. Some use single herbs while others are combinations. Try teas containing chamomile, skullcap passion flower, primrose, hops, catnip, and valerian root. You can also buy ready mixed teas such as Nighty Night, Easy Now and Sleepy Time. One popular combination mixes a spoonful of valerian root, catnip, skullcap, and hops steeped in a pint of boiling water for fifteen minutes. Drink your favorite sleep inducing tea shortly before bedtime.

Herb tablets are a more recent form of sleep remedy. Health food stores carry many tablets for helping you sleep. One particularly effective tablet is called Nature Rest, distributed by American Health, 33 Kings Highway, Orangebury, NY 10962. Nature Rest contains:

500 mg Tryptophan	10 mg Passion Flower
30 mg Valerian Root	10 mg Wild Lettuce
15 mg Chamomile Extract	5 mg B6
15 mg Hops	1 mg B1

<u>Lifestyle Changes</u>. If your personal stress inventory clearly showed that the stresses in your life come from your lifestyle, chances are that your sleep problems stem from the same sources. Changing lifestyles may thus be all it takes to get a good night's sleep.

What To Do If You Can't Get Back To Sleep

If You Prematurely Wake Up From Sleep. Calm yourself immediately. Think thoughts of warmth, heaviness, peacefulness, and relaxation. Let yourself fall gently back into a deep sleep as you think about scenes that deeply relax you. If that doesn't work, get out of bed and leave the bedroom without putting a robe on. When you get cold enough, get back into bed and the warmth of your covers will soon help you drift off.

If You Can't Leave Your Work At Work. Many people lose sleep thinking about their job and work-related problems. You spend enough time at work; if at all possible don't bring it home with you too. Unfortunately, this is easier said than done. The sleep problems caused by work worries usually occur in the early stages of sleep. Your mind comes up with great ideas that you then think about for the rest of the night lying half awake and tense.

If you experience sleeplessness thinking about a new assignment or a big project due, put a tape recorder on your night stand. As soon as the ideas arrive, turn on the tape recorder, don't turn on the light, and record your ideas. Then lie back, take a deep breath, and give a sigh of relief as you fall asleep, content and assured that your wisdom is safely recorded. Try not to wake up completely while recording because it will be more difficult to fall back into your natural sleep cycle.

Work-related sleeplessness is a very common problem that occurs to most people now and then. If it has become a chronic problem, however, you might consider changing your job. Poor sleep will affect your health, family and length of life, and no job is that important. As one U.S. Senator remarked upon quitting the Senate to return home: "I've never heard of a man lying on his death bed saying 'I wished I'd spent more time with my job.'"

Avoid Stimulating Activities. Try not to read a stimulating or frightening story before bedtime or, worse, in an attempt to get back to sleep when you've prematurely awakened. Also avoid reading about sleep problems before bed because you may subconsciously think you have the problem when you don't. Instead read a boring, dry book about subjects that you don't understand or that are of little interest. Technical and computer books work exceptionally well. (Note: this book does not qualify as a boring book.)

Little Black Book. If you lose sleep worrying about forgetting what you have to do the next day keep a detailed, organized appointment book on your night stand. Review the next day's meetings before you go to sleep to reassure yourself that tomorrow is all safely planned.

Muscle Cramps. Muscle cramps can wake you out of a sound sleep. Try more daily exercise, massage, stretching exercises, jacuzzi or a potassium or vitamin E supplement. If none of these suggestions help, see a doctor.

Medical or Psychological Problems. Physical and psychological problems can interfere with the natural sleep process. A reputable hospital sleep clinic can test and evaluate your problem. If you have unexplainable anxiety and depression, lack of self esteem, or experience frequently reoccurring bad dreams, psychological problems quite likely are at fault. A licensed professional counselor or psychiatrist may help you resolve the problems.

CHAPTER 9: RELIEVING THE PAINS OF STRESS

Although stress affects everyone differently, pain is one of the most common consequences. Pain can reduce your concentration, inhibit creativity, lead to increased drug and alcohol use, increase your absenteeism on the job, and impair your ability to function effectively in just about anything you do. However, pain also serves a very valuable purpose. Pain is your body's way of telling you an important message, "we have a problem that has to be taken care of before it gets worse." If you ignore this important message and take medications that suppress the symptoms, without giving so much as a thought as to the cause of the pain, you risk having worse pain later on or even getting a serious physical injury.

Drugs and alcohol are the worst possible methods for coping with pain. They dull the senses, interfere with mental functions, create dependence, and may eventually damage your health while doing nothing to get rid of the original source of pain. There are, however, many safe, natural procedures to help you eliminate pain. Instead of passively accepting chronic pain you can face it, understand it, and then develop your own anti-pain plan.

The first step to eliminating pain is to isolate where it originates in your body and determine its causes. Try to uncover any definite patterns to your problem such as neck pain every time you ride in the car or back pain after sitting in a particular chair. Some everyday factors that may contribute to your pain are: poor posture, excess muscle tension, vertebral misalignment, lack of proper exercise, a chair, mattress or car seat that doesn't provide adequate back support, or disease such as arthritis. Once you know the type of pain and its causes you can begin your campaign against it.

RELIEVING PAIN

The following recommendations for reducing pain are not intended to take the place of proper medical diagnosis and treatment. If you experience severe pain, consult a physician to ensure that your problem is not life threatening such as headaches caused by a brain tumor. Early diagnosis and treatment of a painful disease may mean the difference between life and death. However, if you have non-threatening pains that are being treated with medications that suppress your symptoms but do not eliminate the cause of the problem, try some of the following suggestions for reducing pain.

Improve Your Body Awareness. Postural faults and excess muscle tension can lead to muscle pain and headaches. Become aware of proper posture and the feelings of relaxed muscles. When you feel pains from improper posture or muscle spasms, change your posture or relax the tight muscles as soon as possible. Exercise to keep all your joints mobile, muscles relaxed and flexible, and vertebral column properly aligned. Much pain is simply the result of inactivity. When exercising, be gentle and follow common sense rules about over-exerting yourself. If you bend and lift a lot, use your leg muscles instead of your back muscles.

Heat.

Heat can improve circulation, reduce muscle spasms and pain, and generally relax you. Here are three techniques for applying heat to help reduce pain.

Hot Water - Submerge your body for eight to ten minutes in 102-106° water. If water jets are available, let the pulses hit the most painful points on your body. For overall relaxation, spray tender spots on your feet, ankles, and calves. If you're going to submerge in a hot tub, a few cautions are in order:

Don't drink alcohol before or while in a hot tub.

If possible, avoid being in a hot tub alone; occasionally people fall asleep which can be dangerous.

Do not sit in a hot bath if you are pregnant; the heat can damage the brain of your baby.

If you have uncontrolled high blood pressure, an excessive heart rate, a history of heart problems, or are considerably overweight, consult your doctor before getting into a hot tub.

Stay out of the hot tub if you have a skin disorder, allergy to chlorine, or open wounds.

If you feel faint, get out immediately and take your pulse rate. If the rate is abnormally high for you or the faint feeling persists, call a physician for advice.

If you sprain or bruise a body part, do not place it in hot water for at least 48 hours, or until the swelling goes down and the fever in the area subsides.

Hot Packs (Hydrocollators) - These are gel-filled packs that provide soothing, moist, penetrating deep heat to painful muscles and joints. This type of heat is far more effective at reducing pain than dry heat heating pads that heat only the surface of the body without penetrating into deeper tissue layers. Hot packs are available at pharmacies and medical supply stores. The standard size packs are perfect for the back, hips, and legs; special cervical packs fit the neck and shoulder areas. They're easy to use too. Heat a pack for twenty to thirty minutes in clean, hot $(150-170^{\circ})$ water. Soak new packs in water overnight before using. (Store them in water or in sealed plastic bags in the refrigerator when not in use to prolong their effective life.) Wrap the pack in some towels, then place the pack on the painful area and allow a few minutes for the heat to seep through. Adjust the towel layers for maximum comfort and safety.

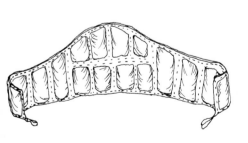

Cervical (Hydrocollators) Hot Pack

Standard Size Hot Pack

Here are a few other hints, and cautions, for using hot packs:

Be careful that you don't burn your hands when lifting them from the water. Use tongs, a pencil, or even a chopstick to pull the pack from the water by one of its loops. Allow the excess water to drop off and then quickly place the pack in a commercially prepared hot pack cover or in a towel. Try not to let the heat escape.

Experiment with different layers of towel until you find the right amount of comfortable heat. Six to eight layers of cotton towel or two to three layers of the thick commercial pack covers between the pack and the skin are usually sufficient. Never lie on a hot pack; it can burn your skin.

Get in a comfortable position when applying a hot pack. You can use a cervical pack while sitting up in a chair or lying down on your abdomen. However, when lying face down don't twist your neck to the side because this will cause muscular imbalances which may add to your pain. If you are most comfortable lying on your stomach, arrange towels or small pillows as a face cradle, or purchase a prone pillow on which you can comfortably place your face down. You may even consider buying a massage table that has a built in face cradle. If you feel back pain while lying on your stomach, a pillow or two under your abdomen takes the strain off your lower back.

Keep the pack on the painful area for twenty to thirty minutes or until it cools. Listen to some relaxing music and practice some of your muscle relaxation exercises. Specially prepared tapes for relaxation and pain control may also be useful.

To relax all of your neck and back muscles, use one cervical pack and as many standard packs as necessary to cover the area from the back of your neck to the bottom of your spine.

Never apply heat to a fresh muscle sprain, bruise, or injury; this will only increase the swelling and lengthen the healing process.

Shower Massage - A wall-mounted or hand-held shower massage is an inexpensive way to relax and relieve pain. Hand-held massagers are more expensive, but are more versatile. To use a shower massager, simply set the water to a comfortably warm temperature and then put the dial on massage-pulse. Concentrate the flow of water on the sorest points on your body.

Ice.

Ice is tremendously effective at reducing pain and swelling that comes from acute sprains, back pain, bursitis, tendonitis, arthritis, shin splints, herniated discs, muscle spasms, and rheumatoid arthritis. To reduce the pain of injuries, apply ice compresses for at least the first forty-eight hours after the injury. Elevate the injured part (such as an ankle) while applying ice packs.

To reduce chronic pain apply ice for 5-15 minutes at a time. The cold decreases nerve conduction, muscle metabolism and sensation which, in turn, helps break the pain cycle. This cycle starts when muscles go into painful spasms that are caused by stress, poor posture, or an injury. The brain senses this pain and responds by trying to protect the muscles by having them spasm even more. The new spasms cause more pain which is then followed by even more spasm. Ice, interrupts this pain cycle and can relax the muscles enough to return them to a normal balance.

You can apply ice with: ice bags (crushed ice works best); ice cups; or even with packages of frozen peas.

Bags full of ice and packages of frozen peas are both effective methods of applying cold to an injury or painful area. Place the bag on the painful area for 5-15 minutes or until the skin becomes white and cold. Use caution if skin sensation is lacking or diminished.

Ice cups are an inexpensive effective way to use ice. To make ice cups, fill paper cups (the six to eight ounce variety) with water and put them in the freezer. (You can also use popsicle sticks or tongue blades as handles.) When you want to use an ice cup take it out of the freezer, and rub your palm over the surface of the ice to remove any sharp points. Then, place the cup on a painful area and move it slowly (about two inches a second) in circular or back and forth motions. Ice applied to the area surrounding the immediate pain area works as well. Don't push the cup down hard, particularly over bones; just let the weight of it touch your skin. Continue this procedure for 5-15 minutes or until the skin is white and the pain has subsided.

Avoid icing if you have Raynauds Disease, are hypersensitive to cold, or if you don't like it. Also avoid icing over an area that has been previously frostbitten.

MASSAGE

Massage is one of the most effective, natural pain control techniques there is. It improves circulation, increases the body's ability to utilize nutrients and eliminate waste products, reduces muscle tension and pain, and helps deeply relax the mind and body. Proper massage will take your mind off problems and will reverse your body's unhealthy physical reactions to stress.

Of the many systems of massage developed over the centuries, the Chinese acupuncture systems recorded over six thousand years ago remains one of the best. Although acupuncture conjures up images of sticking needles into yourself, the massage portion of this science doesn't use needles at all. It's strictly a "hands-on" massage technique.

The Chinese thoroughly studied the body, isolating and recording the points where knots or bands of excessive muscular tension frequently occur. They labelled these points as acupuncture points. Typical acupuncture points indicate injuries, poor posture, inactivity, and unchecked stress, all of which alter the normal balance in muscles and produce pain at the points. The key to reducing, if not entirely eliminating pain, is to consciously relax these points through acupressure.

Acupressure is the touching of sore, tender acupuncture points with your fingers, thumbs, elbows, or whatever else is handy. Pressure directly on the points tells you where they are so you can then relax the specific painful muscles. Relaxing your tender acupressure points will help you break and eliminate the spasm-pain-spasm cycle.

Acupressure is especially helpful if you have no idea where specific points are located or where your pain originates. The pressure and warmth of pressing on these areas helps you tune your mind specifically into these pain centers so that you can relax the right muscles.

Usually massage is a two person affair although, later on, you'll see how to massage yourself.

Two Person Massage Techniques For Eliminating Pain.

For the person receiving the massage:

   Lie on your abdomen with hot packs on your painful points. Lie still for fifteen to twenty minutes while listening to relaxing music or prepared muscle tension relaxation tapes. Take some long, slow, deep, complete breaths and let your mind and body deeply relax as the warmth and moisture from the packs penetrates and soothes your aching muscles (substitute ice if desired).

When the massage begins, focus your entire awareness on how very, very good it feels. Mentally picture your muscle fibers lengthening, unwinding, growing long, loose, limp, and deeply relaxed. Feel your painful points growing warm and heavy, the muscle knots dissolving, and your pain subsiding.

Communicate with the person giving the massage; let the massager know if the pressure is too hard or soft or if the massage is hitting the right spots.

For the person giving the massage:

Warm any massage lotion (vitamin E hand and body lotion works fine) before putting it on the body. Don't shock a relaxed person with cold lotion and hands.

Relax along with your partner and, while relaxing, project thoughts of warmth and heaviness into your hands.

Never apply hard pressure to the neck or low back region. Hard pressure is not needed unless asked for.

Never massage directly on the vertebrae, just on the sides of them.

Try to put your mind into the muscle that you are massaging. Think about what you can do to soothe this muscle to make it relax and feel good.

Have a chart of acupressure points available for reference until you learn the points by heart.

Study your partner's personal stress inventory so that you have an idea of where the most painful points are. However, don't limit your

97

massage to just those areas; other painful points may be going unnoticed.

Massage for the Back, Shoulders and Neck.

Although these techniques are typically used on the back, they work on other areas of the body as well.

Caressing and Gliding. Start at the low back and use soft, gentle, gliding palm strokes up and down the back, along the sides of the vertebral column, all the way to the neck. Don't take your hands off the back as you caress the muscles of the neck, shoulders, gluteals, above and between the shoulder blades and over the shoulder blades. Work very softly at first; as the person relaxes you can use a little more palm pressure as you push up and down and side to side.

Sample Palm Strokes (or invent your own)

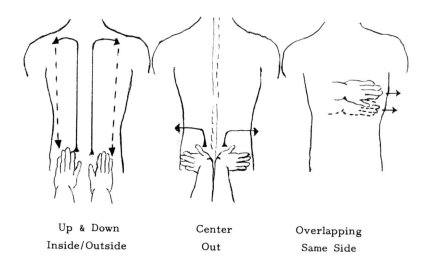

| Up & Down | Center | Overlapping |
| Inside/Outside | Out | Same Side |

Kneading (if the person enjoys it). Gently knead the muscles between the fingers or palms. Squeezing or milking the muscles toward the heart improves the blood flow to and from the muscles.

98

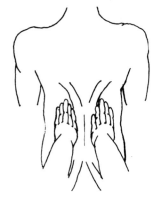 

Kneading Technique A   Kneading Technique B

Thumbs up. Use your thumbs and gently glide them up along side the spinal column, starting at the low back and working your way up to the neck. Repeat this three to six times. Have your partner exhale and relax as you push up. Also glide the thumbs above and along the borders of the shoulder blades. Trace the shoulder blades in this fashion to see where the pain is greatest.

Thumbs out. Start at the same spot on the low back as with thumbs up but now work your way out to the sides of the back. Between the shoulder blades is usually very tender.

Thumb circles. Whenever you come to a tight or tender area, manipulate the knot by moving it side to side, up and down, and by making circles directly over it. Press only as hard as pain will allow.

Sustained pressure. Use your thumbs, knuckles, or elbows to apply direct pressure to a painful area. Use elbows and knuckles when your thumbs tire, but don't press them on bones.

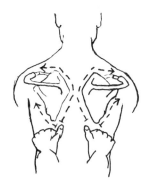

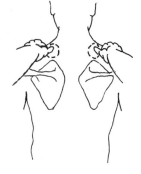

Thumbs Along
Shoulder Blades

Thumb
Circles

<u>Acupressure</u>. Find each point (one at a time) and press hard enough
for your partner to know exactly where the point is. Release the
pressure slightly without moving your finger, thumb, knuckle, or
elbow. Now have your partner take long, slow, deep breaths while
you tell him or her to let the tension flow out with each exhalation.
Tell your partner to picture and feel the muscle relaxing, growing
long, loose, limp and heavy. Keep the pressure on the point until
you feel a pulse indicating that the muscle is relaxing and blood is
flowing to it more freely. To treat most painful points on the back
and between the shoulder blades, push down on the tight points as
hard as comfort will allow (communicate with your partner) and hold
each point until it relaxes. Work your way from the low back to the
base of the neck and then to the muscles on the top of the
shoulders.

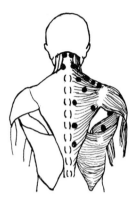

Back of Head, Neck and Shoulders

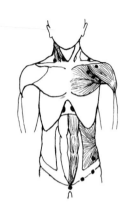

Chest and Abdomen

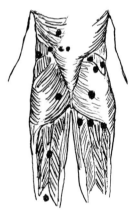

Low Back and Back of Leg

Calf Points

After a while, roll your partner over onto the back. Find the pain points once again and repeat the acupressure technique. Many people can relax more effectively while on their backs. This position is particularly effective for pain points between the shoulder blades, as well as for relieving neck pain, headaches, tight facial, and jaw muscles, and sinus pain points.

To reduce neck pain, gently stroke up along the vertebrae from the base of the neck all the way to the hairline, where you will feel a hole called the Foramen magnum (or acupuncture point 16). Massage the side of the neck, stroking from the shoulders up to the ears and jaw. Next, massage the muscles from the vertebrae out to the sides of the neck working up from the bottom to the top of the neck. When you get to the hairline, massage above and all around point 16 searching for tender areas.

If you find a tender area, hold it while your partner breathes deeply and tries to consciously relax the muscles of the area. Next, stroke along the hairline from point 16 to the backs of the ears, doing the same relaxing and breathing exercises at each tight point. Tilt your partner's chin slightly up as you place your middle fingers on each side of the hairline by point 16. Gently pull your partner's head towards you and hold it for twenty seconds. This gentle traction relieves pressure from the neck muscles and nerve routes. If you are apprehensive about trying this technique, the pillow in the illustration provides the same type of cervical traction.

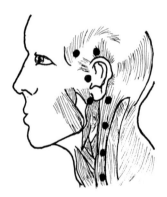

Side of the Head and Neck Points   Cervical Traction Pillow

With your partner still lying face up, massage down the front of both ears, paying particular attention to the temporal mandibular joints located just in front of the ear holes. Continue this gentle massage below the ear lobes and then progress along the bottom of the jaw bone until your fingers meet at the bottom of the chin.

Next, massage the forehead and temples and work your way back across the hair to a point above the ears, always searching for tight, tender muscles. Lightly massage the scalp and then massage the eyebrows and cheeks. If you have an acupressure chart handy touch the facial points listed on the chart. Hold each point gently for fifteen seconds and then put both hands on the back of your partner's neck for ten seconds thinking thoughts of warmth and relaxation.

To reduce painful points on the back and between the shoulder blades, have your partner push down on your upward facing fingers (located on the pain points) as hard as is comfortable. Hold each point until it relaxes.

Now have your partner sit up into a comfortable, correct posture position. To make sure the posture is right, roll a towel up and place it behind the low back, or alternatively, use a specially designed back cushion.

Low Back Cushion   Full Back Cushion

Sitting behind your partner, gently run your fingers or thumbs up and down the sides of the vertebrae, between and above the shoulder blades, and along the tops of the shoulders. Touch each of the neck and shoulder acupressure points once again for ten to fifteen seconds. When you have finished, grasp the upper arms and have the person breathe in fully and relax as you manually raise the shoulders up and back, gently squeezing the shoulder blades together and stretching the chest muscles. Then have your partner exhale as slowly as possible as you lower the shoulders as slowly as possible. Repeat this three times. Finally rest your hands on the neck and shoulders for ten to fifteen seconds projecting warmth and relaxation.

If the severe pain still persists after this treatment, the pain is probably from a vertebrae out of alignment. A misaligned vertebrae places pressure on the nerves and causes muscles to spasm and become painful. A visit to a doctor or chiropractor is in order. A chiropractor's specialty is restoring the vertebral column to its proper positioning. If you do get your spine re-adjusted, start a program of proper exercise to improve your posture and body awareness. At the same time, practicing deep relaxation will relax tight muscles and help to keep your body aligned correctly.

Self Massage

If you can reach them, you can massage the acupressure points on your own body. The following techniques will help relieve pain and relax your muscles.

Place a pillow on a table in front of you, sit down in a chair, and rest your face in the pillow. Raise one arm over the top and massage the back of your head, neck, shoulders, and whatever other points you can reach. Repeat with the other arm.

Lie on your side, reach over your shoulders and massage in between your shoulder blades. Reach up from your waist to reach your lower back.

To massage your legs and feet, as well as your back, sit in a chair or on a bed with your back against the headboard.

Lie flat on your back to massage tight neck and back muscles.

Put two tennis balls in a sock and tie the end of the sock. Lie on your back and roll the the balls over your painful muscles.

When you get out of the shower, firmly and briskly dry your whole body.

Foot Massage - your poor feet. You suffocate them in socks, cram them in shoes, pound them on hard pavement, and probably spend little time caring for them. Foot massage can improve circulation, reduce pain and produce an overall feeling of relaxation in your body. Here's the foot massage technique:

Wash your feet in warm water and soap, and dry them well. Place a small amount of hand lotion or cream on your hands. Squeeze one foot, starting at the toes and working towards the ankles. Rub your hands over the sole and top of the foot and then run your knuckles firmly along the sole starting at the base of the toes and working towards the heels. Push your thumbs in small circles along the full length of the sole, searching for painful points. Don't neglect behind the toes, the ball of the foot and the arch. Bend the toes forward and back and side to side and rub between each toe. Squeeze the tip of each toe and then give each a gentle pull with your thumbs on the nail. Run both thumbs down each of the grooves on top of your foot while pushing your fingers up from the sole into the same groove. In each groove, gently separate and roll your foot bones up and down. Start at the groove separating the big toe from the second toe and work towards the little toe, separating all of the bones. Pinch your Achilles tendon between your thumb and index finger, searching for painful areas. If you find a painful spot, gently pinch it and then press on it from the back. Massage the top of your ankle working up to your calf. Finally, put one hand on top of your foot and the other on the bottom. Think about heat, warmth and relaxation for ten to fifteen seconds. Now, feel the difference between your feet. Repeat the massage on the other foot.

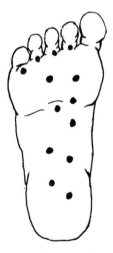

Foot Massage Points

BIOFEEDBACK

Biofeedback is a stress reduction technique that can help relax muscles, reduce tension and anxiety, and even eliminate painful headaches. The biofeedback process starts by measuring muscle tension and hand temperature because tense muscles and cold hands are generally good indicators of stress. To make those measurements you attach an electromyometer (EMM) to some tense muscles and a digital thermometer to one finger tip. The EMM has a dial that shows muscle tension in microvolts of electricity and the digital thermometer reads the normal degrees Fahrenheit. So far, so good. Now comes the crux of biofeedback. While watching the EMM dial you concentrate on making your muscle relax. At first, nothing may happen because you're either not concentrating enough or you're not thinking about relaxing the right way. The needle on the dial doesn't move. But then, as you discover the right way to relax the muscles, the needle begins to fall, slowly at first and then more rapidly as you master the technique. Being able to see the dial move in direct response to your own thoughts is the -feedback part of biofeedback.

As you become proficient in biofeedback you'll be able to make the needle move down, up, hold steady, or swing back and forth. You have, at that point, complete control over your muscles. You can then learn the same technique to control hand warmth by watching temperature readings on the hand thermometer change as you concentrate on making your hands warmer or cooler. With these two skills, you've gained an enormously efficient way to reduce stress.

You can use the muscle relaxing feedback to reduce the tightness of a particular muscle in any part of your body. It's especially effective for relaxing the frontalis muscles (in your forehead) that cause headaches and pain when they're tight. Temperature feedback is effective for reducing overall tension, but more significantly it's been found to work exceptionally well for people suffering from migraine headaches, hypertension, Burger's disease, Raynaud's disease, diabetes, high blood pressure, and anxiety syndrome. Imagine at the onset of a migraine headache being able to reverse the symptoms and relax your body. That's what biofeedback is all about.

There are a number of different types of biofeedback equipment. Some EMM's and thermometers produce a sound as well as a dial reading. For instance, one EMM produces a low tone that corresponds to the tension of the muscle it's attached to. As you mentally relax the muscle, the tone becomes softer and softer and the dial falls at the same time. Having both the visual and auditory feedback helps you learn biofeedback faster and, according to some biofeedback experts, also helps you focus more fully on relaxing a particular set of muscles. Some digital thermometers also produce sounds corresponding to hand temperature readings.

Once you've learned the biofeedback technique, does that mean you've got to have an EMM or thermometer in your pocket whenever you want to relax? Not at all. You'll be able to concentrate to relax muscles and warm hands during meetings, while riding on an airplane or in a taxi, at your work desk, or at any time or place you can devote your mind fully to reducing your stresses. Don't sell the equipment though. You'll occasionally need a "refresher" or "tune-up" session to sharpen up your biofeedback abilities. You may also find the equipment useful when you're under severe stress and tension and just can't seem to concentrate correctly. Those times, more than any other, are when you'll be glad you learned biofeedback. (See the back of the book for information to order inexpensive biofeedback equipment.)

RELIEF FROM HEADACHES

Virtually 100% of the people in the world have had a headache at one time or another. About 90% of those headaches are caused by tension; roughly 8% are migraines. Stress reduction can help in both of these cases, however, if you suffer very severe headaches, see your doctor first to find out if there is some other cause (such as illness or a brain tumor).

Tension headaches are usually caused by poor posture, excessive tension and painful trigger points in the muscles of the neck, shoulders, forehead and side of the head, teeth grinding, eye strain, and a painful jaw (known as temporal mandibular joint syndrome).

Migraine headaches are caused by too much blood in the blood vessels of the brain. For this reason migraines are also referred to as vascular (blood-vessel) headaches. The excess blood causes pressure against the meninges (membranes that cover the brain) which results in migraine pain.

Learning to decrease the abnormal pooling of blood in the brain will help you naturally eliminate your headaches. Stress, food allergies, hormonal imbalances, viruses, hangovers, and painful trigger points are the suspected causes of migraines.

Here's how to relieve yourself of most headaches:

Always maintain proper neck and shoulder posture.

Recognize and relax tight neck, shoulder, scalp and facial muscles. Use heat or ice, massage, acupressure, deep relaxation and muscle awareness exercises.

Press and relax the headache relief acupressure points.

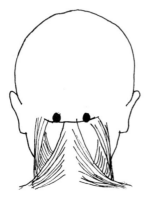

Back of Head and Neck

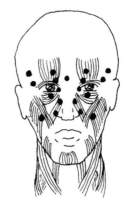

Facial and Eye Points

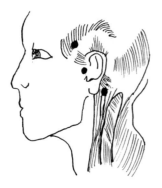

Side of the Head

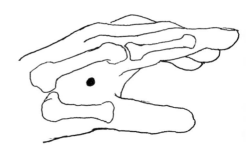

Hoku Point

Check your temporal mandibular joint (TMJ) by placing your index finger tips in the notches right in front of your ear canals. Then slowly open and close your jaw. If you experience pain, muscle spasms or perceive a clicking in the joint, it may be out of alignment and causing your headaches.

Dentists specializing in TMJ problems can tell if you need a MORA (Mandibular Orthopedic Repositioning Appliance) which realigns the jaw, positioning it properly with the rest of your skull bones. The MORA is worn on the bottom teeth and does not interfere with eating or talking. It may be your end to aspirins.

The next time you have a headache check the temperature of your hands. If they are cold there is a good chance your headache is being caused by too much blood in the blood vessels of your brain. Warming your hands through biofeedback or autogenic suggestions shifts the blood to the hands from the brain and can eliminate your headache.

Autogenic exercises use passive suggestions of warmth and heaviness to raise hand and foot temperature and relieve migraine headaches. Chapter 7 describes autogenic exercises. If you have a headache or feel one coming on, lie or sit down in a quiet comfortable place, take some long, slow deep breaths, relax, and use the autogenic suggestions to passively tell your hands and feet to warm up.

Exercises to relieve headaches caused by eye strain

Sometimes your headaches come from eye strain and fatigue that lead to excess muscle tension. The following set of eye exercises can reduce the strain and tension, and relieve your headaches. While performing these exercises only move your eyes, not your head.

Look straight ahead and roll your eyes upwards as far as they will go. Hold them up for five seconds and then return them to straight ahead.

Look down towards the floor, rolling your eyes as far as they will go. Hold them there for five seconds.

Roll your eyes to the right for five seconds and return to straight ahead. Repeat to the left.

Roll your eyes in the largest clockwise circles you can make. Repeat three times. Repeat in the counter-clockwise direction.

Close your eyes and press gently inward on them for five seconds.

Massage all around your eye sockets. Then, press each of the eye acupressure points (see the acupressure chart) for ten to fifteen seconds. Spend extra time on any painful points you find.

Headaches may also occur after you eat excessive amounts of white sugar, alcoholic beverages, food coloring, preservatives, artificial ingredients, and foods that you're allergic to. Keep track of your diet to see if there is a pattern between the foods you eat and the frequency of headaches. If you suspect that your diet is causing headaches, read the next chapter for recommendations and suggestions concerning food.

CHAPTER 10: DIET AND STRESS

Most people don't think twice about how their diet affects their health. This is unfortunate because a poor diet can bring on obesity, cardiovascular disease, high blood pressure, diabetes, insomnia, cancer, allergies, muscle tension, softening of the bones, depression, a poor self-image, constipation, headaches, and stress. Although no single diet is adequate for everyone, following certain dietary principles will improve your health and eliminate some of your stress.

Diets are all the rage these days. Some of the more popular mass market books about diets are: the Beverly Hills Diet, the Pritikin Diet, Stress and Nutrition, Weight Watchers, Dr. Atkins' Diet, and Eat to Win. The main problem with the diets presented in these books is that they're one diet that's supposed to work for everyone. If you've tried any of them ask yourself these questions: "Did you lose (or gain) weight? Did you re-gain it later? and, Did staying on the diet produce stress to stick with the diet plan?" The plain fact is that being on a fad diet is, itself, a stress. That's one more stress you just don't need.

Before starting on a stress-reducing diet, the first order of business is to make sure that the diet fulfills all of your nutritional needs. Next is to realize how diets work: 1) most quick weight loss comes from the loss of muscle and water, not fat; 2) when you lose fat you lose it from over your entire body, not just in a particular area.

A good nutritional program is one that maintains or achieves your ideal body weight while providing all of the nutrients essential for good health. Ideal body weight refers to the optimal percentage of body fat which for men is 15-20%, and for women is 18-24%. The population average for American men is 25% fat and for women is 28-30% fat. Finding out your percentage of body fat is no simple chore, however. The preferred method at hospitals and weight clinics is to compare your normal weight with your weight when under water. In addition, a technique recently developed measures your body fat with low voltage electrical currents. You can also simply look in the mirror without holding your gut in and be honest with yourself.

So, how do you eat to reduce stress? Refer back to your PSI. In the question about nutrition, Diet A contains the general recommendations of nutritionists. But those are only broad guidelines to follow. It's up to you to develop your own diet for your body, metabolism, energy level, and lifestyle. As long as your diet fits within these recommendations, you're on your way to healthy, stress-free eating. And if you selected one of the other PSI diets -- Diet B - junk-food, Diet C - meat and potatoes or Diet D - vegetarian -- what can you do? If you selected Diet B and don't change your eating habits, at least keep your life insurance up to date. That way your deadly self-abuse will have some benefit for your next of kin. For Diet C, prepare yourself for a life of bowel problems, hardened arteries and increased risk of heart attack.

If you choose Diet D, learn to balance your meals to get the right combination of amino acids. For your body to obtain the right balance of protein from foods, you need to ingest all nine essential amino acids. However, three of the amino acids, known as limiting acids, are particularly important because without them the other six are useless, even if available in the right quantities. Very few vegetarian foods contain all nine of the amino acids, thus it's crucial to balance your meals appropriately. An excellent vegetarian cookbook that describes the amino acids balance is Laurel's Kitchen (Nilgiri Press, Berkeley, California). Check with a nutritionist if you have other questions. Often, your county health service will also answer your nutrition inquiries.

Vitamin balance in a vegetarian diet is also important. Vitamin B12 deficiency is a common flaw in many vegetarian diets.

Overall, vegetarian diets can be healthy and life-prolonging. They just take a little more planning than a burger and fries.

THE STRESS REDUCTION DIET / A HEALTHY WAY TO EAT

Choose a variety of foods from all four food groups. Eating a variety decreases the possibility that you will develop a deficiency (or excess) of one nutrient.

Milk - Consume two or three cups of these products each day. Eating non-fat milk or yogurt and low fat cheese reduces fat intake.

Protein - Protein should make up roughly 25% of your diet. Increase consumption of white fish, skinned poultry, and vegetable sources of protein such as tofu, legumes, grains and seeds. These less fatty sources of protein are healthier because they reduce your risk of getting heart disease. Reduce your meat and pork consumption to two to three times a week.

Fruits and vegetables - Eat at least four servings of fruit and vegetables each day. Vary the colors and types. Select fresh products whenever possible. When you must use frozen or canned products, buy fruit without added sweeteners and vegetables without added salt or sauces. Eat vegetables raw or steam them only briefly keeping them crisp; overcooking removes the nutrients.

Breads and cereals - Select breads, cereals, and pasta products made from whole grains. These and other complex carbohydrates, such as potatoes and brown rice, provide fiber, which helps prevent constipation and other more serious bowel disorders.

GENERAL TIPS FOR REDUCING FOOD INDUCED STRESS

Eliminate caffeine from your diet. Typical caffeine-rich foods are coffee, tea, chocolate, and soda pop. If you are highly stressed, caffeine--very powerful in its own right--will arouse your already overactive nervous system and, in essence, will compound your problems. Try drinking herbal teas and/or beverages that have no caffeine.

Eliminate or drastically cut back on sugar in your diet. Eating foods having a high percentage of sugar produces dramatic blood sugar level fluctuations that may lead to between-meal hunger, sluggishness, and irritability. White and brown sugar, honey, syrups, candy bars, doughnuts, pastries, cookies, and ice cream all produce a sugar rush of

113

energy that quickly brings you up, lasts for a brief period of time, and then drops you down in the dumps. When you come down off your "sugar high" there is also a greater tendency to snack on more sugar to quickly bring yourself back up once again. Think of it this way: one piece of chocolate is too many and a million aren't enough.

Misuse of sugar products can also lead to tooth decay, increased body fat, and diabetes. Fruit is a much better way to take in sugar. Fruit gradually releases sugars into your system; your increased energy level remains up for a longer period of time, and then gently dissipates without any withdrawal symptoms. Fruit also is a good source of fiber.

To illustrate your daily intake of sugar, do this: take 21 teaspoons of sugar out of your sugar jar and put them on a plate. If you eat the average American diet, that's how much sugar you eat each day. Each and every day! Now, think again about cutting down on sugar.

Reduce consumption of salt and foods high in salt. Too much salt (sodium, sodium nitrate, sodium benzoate and monosodium glutamate [msg]) in your diet, and hence too much sodium in your body, may lead to high blood pressure which in turn increases the risk of stroke, heart attack, and kidney damage.

Although many foods don't taste salty, they are. For example, seafood, dairy products (including cheese), canned vegetables and soup, baked goods, and cereals are all loaded with salt or salt additives. In fact, one fast food meal alone may account for half your daily salt needs. As an alternative to salt, experiment with lemon juice, lime juice, garlic, fresh ginger, dill, tarragon, and other spices to enhance the flavor of food without endangering your health.

Avoid fatty and greasy foods. These foods tremendously increase your chance of experiencing cardiovascular disease. No more than 30% of your total calories should come from fat and at least half of your total fat intake should come from unsaturated fat sources such as corn, safflower, soybean, and sesame oils. Lowering your cholesterol level 10 to 15% by cutting down on fat and cholesterol, can reduce your chance of having a fatal heart attack by 20 to 30%. A low fat diet is even more important if you're under stress because blood cholesterol levels increase during peak periods of stress.

If you think you have a high cholesterol level (or score above 190 on a blood test), restructure your diet away from animal fats found in greasy meats, and the "invisible" fat found in products such as mayonnaise, butter and cheese, eggs, potato chips, olives, nuts, and chocolate. When preparing your meals, broil or bake foods instead of frying them. Also, eat more high fiber foods such as oats, dried beans and peas, and fruits. These foods can actually lower cholesterol levels by increasing the levels of high density lipoproteins (HDLs) in your blood. HDLs purge the arteries of low density lipoproteins (LDLs), the glue-like substances that make artery walls sticky enough for plaque (floating fat) to adhere and build up, choking off your flow of life sustaining blood. In addition to eating less fat, aerobic exercising increases your level of cleansing HDLs.

Try to balance your caloric intake with your energy expenditure. For instance, if you lead a sedentary life, cut down on the amounts you eat. The excess food simply becomes stored fat. Beginning around the age of 25 your body needs less and less food each year. A rule of thumb is that you need about 10,000 calories less per year, or about 25 less calories per day, each year. Of course, if you increase your exercise, or get a more physical job, your caloric requirements may increase. All else being equal, though, the older you get, the less you should eat. And as you eat less, the balance of your diet becomes even more important.

Reduce alcohol consumption. Alcoholic beverages are high in calories and low in nutrients. Excessive indulgence can alter the way your body absorbs and uses food; too much alcohol can also impair sleep quality and lead to very serious health problems. Try mineral water, spring water, or natural fruit juices as healthier alternatives.

Eat wisely, not blindly. Are you omniverous (eat everything and anything in sight) and do you eat out of habit? The next time you sneak to the refrigerator, ask yourself the following questions: "Am I really hungry? Do I need to eat? Is the food nutritious? How will I feel after I've eaten?" Learning to say no to food when you aren't hungry is a giant step in the right direction.

Some other "eat wise" suggestions: eat foods that make you feel good and avoid foods that upset your system. You may be allergic to some foods or cannot digest them properly. Avoid artificial ingredients such as food coloring, preservatives, and flavor enhancers; stick to the real thing. The next time you feel sick, think about what you ate recently.

Chew your food well. Many people under heavy stress bolt their food down and do not take the time to chew it adequately. Take the time to savor each bite. Not only will this help you stop rushing for a few moments, it will also make your digestive tract's job much easier.

Do you need vitamin supplements? It depends. If you're healthy and you eat well, the answer is no. If you don't eat well and are subject to a high degree of stress, absolutely yes. Vitamins help your body perform functions essential to health and life. Without them you can suffer all sorts of malodies ranging from scurvy (lack of vitamin C) to a general malaise and feeling of discomfort.

Fat soluble vitamins, A, D, E, and K, dissolve in fats and are stored in the body. Conversely, water soluble vitamins, including C, B (Thiamine), B2 (Riboflavin), B3 (Niacin), B6 (Pyridoxine), B12 (Cobalmin), Folic Acid, Biotin, and Panthothenic Acid are not stored in the body and must be included in your daily diet.

Stress, smoking, air pollution, drug and alcohol use, aging, infections, and burn wounds all increase your body's demand for vitamins. Studies have shown that if you smoke, drink, use drugs, or are subject to severe stress you should supplement your daily diet with a formula comparable to the following:

Vitamin C	600 mg.
Vitamin B1	20 mg.
Vitamin B2	15 mg.
Vitamin B6	25 mg.
Vitamin B12	25 mcg.
Niacinamide	100 mg.
Panthothenic acid	30 mg.
Folic Acid	400 mcg.
Vitamin E	45 I.U.
Biotin	100 mcg.
Zinc	30 mg.
Magnesium	75 mg.

One note of caution: treat vitamins as you would any other drug. The old philosophy that if some is good more is better, is not true for vitamins. Excessive vitamin intake can disrupt your metabolism, affect your hormone levels, cause sensory damage (blindness and, in some cases, can even be fatal). Don't exceed recommended doses and don't take vitamins if you are taking prescription drugs.

DIET, HEART ATTACK, AND STROKE

The factors in your diet, lifestyle, and heredity may contribute to your risk of having a heart attack or stroke. If you want to assess your own individual risk, here's a quick test.

Heart Attack and Stroke Risk Self Appraisal

1. Male _____   Female _____
2. Age _____
3. If you are overweight, estimate how many pounds over your ideal weight you are at this moment.
   0-5 lbs. _____   5-10 lbs. _____   10-20 lbs. _____   20-30 lbs. _____
   More than 30 lbs. _____
4. Do you smoke? Yes _____   No _____
   If yes, estimate how many cigarettes you smoke each day: _____
5. Has any member of your immediate family died of a heart attack before the age of 65? Yes _____   No _____
6. Do you eat red meat 6 or more times a week? Yes _____   No _____
7. Do you eat organ meats (liver, kidneys, etc.) more than once a month? Yes _____   No _____
8. Do you eat 5 or more eggs a week? Yes _____   No _____
9. Do you eat hog dogs, cold cuts, or luncheon meats 3 to 5 times a week? Yes _____   No _____
10. Do you consume whole milk, cheese, or ice cream 3 to 5 times a week? Yes _____   No _____
11. Do you eat deep fat fried foods about 3 to 5 times a week? Yes _____
    No _____
12. Do you use mayonnaise and butter 3 to 5 times a week? Yes _____
    No _____
13. Do you frequently enjoy sweets every day (sugar or honey in your hot drinks, soda, candy, jelly, cake, cookies, etc.)? Yes _____
    No _____

117

14. How often do you exercise aerobically? Never ____ Sometimes ____
    Vigorously for at least twenty, non-stop minutes 3 times a week ____
15. Do you always add salt to your food? Yes ____ No ____
16. Do you practice some form of deep relaxation at least 3 times a week?
    Yes ____ No ____
17. Is your life full of deadline and time pressures? Yes ____ No ____
18. Select the category that the first number of your most recent blood
    pressure measurement falls into:
    119 or less ____ between 120 and 139 ____ between 140 and
    159 ____ 160 or above ____

What to do with the results!

1. ____ Score 1 point if you are a man; 0 points if you are a
   woman.
2. ____ Add 1 point if you are over 35.
3. ____ Add 1 point for every ten pounds that you are over
   weight.
   5-10 lbs. = 1 pt. 10-20 lbs. = 2 pts. 20-30 lbs. = 3
   pts. More than 30 lbs. = 4 pts. (Even someone 50 lbs.
   over will just get 4 pts.)
4. ____ Add 0 points if you don't smoke; add 1 point for each 1/2
   pack you smoke each day.
5. ____ Add 1 point for each member of your immediate family who
   died of a heart attack or stroke before the age of 65.
6. ____ Add 1 point if you eat red meat 6 or more times a week.
7. ____ Add 1 point if you eat organ meats once a month.
8. ____ Add 1 point if you eat 5 or more eggs a week.
9-13. ____ For these questions, add 1 point for up to 2 yes answers
   and 2 points for 3 or more yes responses.
14. ____ Subtract 1 point if you exercise 20 minutes 3 times a week;
   add 1 point if you get some exercise; add 2 points if you
   do not exercise.
15. ____ Add 1 point if you always add salt to your food.
16. ____ Subtract 1 point if you practice deep relaxation 3 times a
   week. Add 0 points if you don't.
17. ____ Add 1 point if your life is full of deadline and time
   pressures.

18.   _____   Subtract 1 point for 119 or less; Add 0 points for between 120 and 139; add 1 point for between 140 and 159; and add 2 points for 160 or above.

_____   TOTAL

Now, total the points up and compare your results to the corresponding statement below.

0 - 4   Congratulations! A score of 4 or less indicates that for your age and sex you have a very low risk of experiencing a heart attack or stroke.

5 - 7   Your score in this range indicates that you demonstrate a below average risk of having a heart attack or stroke. However, you may want to modify certain aspects of your life to either decrease or maintain your risk at this level.

8 - 10   Your score in this range indicates that you have an average risk of experiencing a heart attack or stroke. Have your physician give you a stress test. Ask about changes in diet, exercise, and lifestyle that can lower the risk. Become serious about sticking to your personal stress reduction plan so you don't slip into the high risk category.

11 - 13   You have a high risk of experiencing a heart attack or stroke. Have a complete medical check-up including a stress test, a percent of body fat test, and blood analysis to assess cholesterol, triglyceride (blood fat) and lipoprotein levels. Adhere to your physician's recommendations and stick with your personal stress reduction program.

Above 14   Danger! You have an extremely high risk of having a heart attack or stroke. Have a complete medical checkup immediately! Make sure the checkup includes a stress test, a percent of body fat test, and blood analysis to assess your cholesterol, triglyceride (blood fat), and lipoprotein levels. Your doctor will advise you of essential changes to your diet, exercise and lifestyle that you must make to stay alive. Your personal stress reduction program is more important than ever.

OTHER DIET AND STRESS RECOMMENDATIONS

If you have high blood pressure - stop using salt, reduce consumption of fat and cholesterol, if you are overweight, lose weight, stop smoking, avoid drinking to excess, stop eating sugar and sweets, eliminate caffeine from your diet, exercise more, practice focused breathing and deep relaxation and stick with your personal stress reduction program.

If you have a history of cardiovascular problems - follow the dietary recommendations outlined in this chapter. Reduce your weight to your ideal body weight, stop using salt, eat less food high in fat and cholesterol, stop smoking, avoid sugar and sweets, cut way down on your alcohol consumption, avoid caffeine, regularly practice aerobic exercise, deep relaxation, and focused breathing. Stick with your personal stress reduction plan.

If you have an ulcer or digestive problems - avoid acidic foods, eat more fiber, avoid caffeine, and chew your food very well. Practice deep relaxation of your abdominal muscles and visual imagery for problem healing.

If you have headaches - they may be caused by food allergies. Study them to see if any pattern exists between the foods you eat and frequency of the headaches. A physician specializing in allergies can test for allergic reactions to a wide variety of foods and other substances. Refer to the chapter on reducing the pains of stress for more information on controlling headaches.

If you have muscle spasms - calcium and magnesium are natural muscle relaxants. In addition, a commercially available mixture, known as dc Formula 303 is tremendously effective at reducing muscle tension and spasms. Available from DEE CEE Laboratories, Madison, TN 37115, it contains valerian root, passiflora powder extracts, and magnesium. Muscle cramps could also be caused by the lack of potassium. Eat more bananas or take a potassium supplement. Refer to the chapter on reducing the pains of stress for more information.

If you have problems sleeping - L-Tryptophan (500 mg.) is a naturally occurring amino acid, found in turkey and other protein sources, that helps induce sleep. Calcium and magnesium, dc Formula 303 and herbal teas are also effective sleep aids. Refer to the chapter on sleep improvement for more detailed information on how to get a good night's sleep.

If you are susceptible to minor illnesses or experience chronic fatigue - your best bet is to have a complete physical and blood evaluation by your physician. If you're physically sound then the problem could be your diet. Have a nutritionist thoroughly evaluate your eating habits. Closely follow the diet recommendations and keep track of your illnesses and energy levels. If they don't improve it may be possible that unchecked stress is the culprit. Get more exercise, frequently practice deep relaxation and diaphragmatic breathing exercises, think about making the lifestyle changes called for in your personal stress reduction plan.

CHAPTER 11: MORE TIPS FOR MANAGING YOUR STRESS

This chapter contains additional information to help you cope more effectively with your daily stress. Not all of the tips may apply to you today. Some may become important later when you receive stresses you've never thought about. Glance over all this material so you'll know where to turn whenever new stresses rear their ugly heads.

NOT ENOUGH TIME IN THE DAY

Timelessness is not having enough time in the day to do everything you need to do or want to accomplish. Timlessness is a major cause of stress in our frantic world. People constantly run from one project to the next without ever taking time to rest, to think their own thoughts, enjoy the beauty of a sunset, marvel at a flower, or spend time with family and loved ones. Unlike a simple hamster that jumps off its tread wheel when it's tired, many human beings obsessed with work, money, fame, prestige, and power cast aside logic and reason and literally work themselves to death. You can avoid this "hurry sickness syndrome", reduce your stress, and add quality to your life by learning how to get the most out of your time.

Using Time More Effectively

Organize your life. Every day record a list of what you want and need to accomplish. Separate events, appointments, and tasks into priorities. Take care of the most urgent and critical matters first. When you complete a job on the list, give yourself a pat on the back and take some time for yourself. Tasks impossible to finish should be carried over to the next day's list. Don't put matters off too long because unfinished business can be stressful and take its toll on your mind and body. Be very careful when making the list to set realistic, attainable goals, otherwise asking too much from yourself will create stress and frustration.

Handle each piece of paper as little as possible. Separate your paperwork into three groups: 1) urgent and top priority; 2) tasks that need to be done soon; and 3) trivial pursuits (for when you have nothing else to do). Don't procrastinate with your paperwork, get it done and get on to your next task.

Use your time wisely. Study your behavior to determine the time of day that you work most effectively. For instance, if you write your best in the morning, schedule your writing then and leave the rest of the day for other jobs. Schedule your time according to your personality.

Learn to say No. Some people accept too much responsibility. Learn your limitations and capabilities. If you spread yourself too thin your work performance and health will suffer. Assert yourself, take care of yourself, and if you really don't want to do something, or have the time to do it, don't.

Take time out. When you feel yourself getting out of control, call a time out. Rearrange your schedule to have some time for relaxing and recharging your energy. If you can't spare the time to have some fun and relax, deep relaxation is your only healthy alternative. Wake up a few minutes early and do some deep relaxation first thing in the morning, or listen to a relaxation tape during your coffee break, or at lunch. Regardless of when you practice deep relaxation, it will help break the stresses of constantly rushing through life. Believe it or not, taking time for yourself improves your productivity and reduces the amount of time it takes you to get a job done.

Unclouding your thoughts. If you are having difficulty thinking clearly, step back from your daily routine, look at your life, and objectively (and honestly) determine the cause of your fuzzy thoughts. Is it a work overload, the medication you're taking to reduce your blood pressure or muscle tension, lack of sleep, drug or alcohol abuse, or the inability to cope with your stress? Once you isolate the cause of your problem you can eliminate it. Then, with clear eyes and sharp thoughts you can get your jobs done in a fraction of the time it might have taken you.

Generally, you should avoid caffeine, chemical sleeping pills and muscle relaxants. Follow the suggestions in Chapter 8 for improving your sleep, practice focused breathing and deep relaxation, exercise more, seek professional help for a drug and/or alcohol problem, consider changing jobs, and follow your personal stress reduction plan.

COPING WITH PSYCHOLOGICAL
AND SOCIAL STRESS

The psychological and social manifestations of stress are often the most debilitating. Inability to cope with stress may interfere with mental health and happiness, impair ability to raise a family, erode social and work relationships, reduce job performance, and damage your physical health. If for no apparent reason you frequently experience anxiety, irritability, strained relationships, easily aroused hostility, depression, trouble turning off the mind at night, stressful dreams, low motivation, pessimism, worrying, lack of control over your life, a short fused temper, or drug and alcohol abuse, it is absolutely essential that you unearth what is causing the problems and then take action to eliminate them.

Getting to the root of your problems
Pinpointing the causes of your chronic psycho-social stress symptoms is the first step to eliminating them. This, however, is much easier said than done. Uncovering the information demands that you thoroughly analyze your behavior and life with an open mind. Take an in-depth look at each of your problems and try to figure out why you're reacting to your stress the way you are. There's no magical way to do this. Simply sit quietly and think about your problems and their causes. Be honest and thorough, and above all, be patient with yourself. Enough people in the world are quick to be hostile to you.

Start by re-evaluating your goals and aspirations in life. You may have set your sights unrealistically high and are putting too much pressure on yourself. Work through each problem until you see its cause clearly. If you just can't come face to face with the cause of your problems, consider speaking to a counselor who is skilled in solving personal problems.

Forget the misconception that you're crazy if you seek help for a psychological problem. It takes a person with confidence to realize that some problems need professional help. After your problems are fully diagnosed, determine the best course of action for reducing your stress. For many people, living a less stressful life demands changes in job and lifestyle.

Job and Lifestyle Changes

Sometimes taking a long, hard look at your life is the best way to determine the most beneficial course of action. Ask yourself: "What do I want to do with my life?" Frequently, an honest answer requires job or lifestyle changes. For instance, if you're a workaholic (and can't stop working or thinking about work) your hard work pays the bills, but is it worth jeopardizing your health and relationship with your family? If you suspect this, or other problems in your life, use the following survey to determine how satisfied you are with your present vocation and lifestyle.

JOB/LIFESTYLE SURVEY

		Yes	No
1)	Are you happy with your job? Lifestyle?	___	___
2)	Do you make enough money for what you do?	___	___
3)	Do you have a realistic chance for doing better?	___	___
4)	Do you get along well with your colleagues, family and friends?	___	___
5)	Do you feel part of the work team?	___	___
6)	Do you feel love at home?	___	___
7)	Are you overloaded with work?	___	___
8)	Do you take time for your family?	___	___
9)	Are you burned out (have lost enthusiasm for your job)?	___	___
10)	Do you need new challenges?	___	___
11)	Do you feel a change of jobs would help?	___	___

12) What are the risks if you don't change?

_____

_____

13) What are the risks if you do change?

_____

_____

14) Is there time to find a better solution? If no, why not?

_____

_____

15) What are your possible courses of action?

_____

_____

_____

_____

_____

_____

_____

_____

Now look back through this brief survey. Do you honestly think a job or lifestyle change is appropriate. Or are you willing to continue with your current situation. The purpose of this survey is simply to lay out your complaints clearly. It's up to you to decide if action is the answer. If you do decide to change, read the next section "Effective Decision Making" to reduce the stresses brought about by your choices.

Effective Decision-Making

When making critical decisions about your lifestyle or job (i.e., managing money, changing jobs, buying a home, investments, moving, ...,) a "decision balance sheet" can often help clarify the preferred choices. Using the balance sheet method you can make a side-by-side comparison of the positive and negative aspects of each alternative choice.

Directions: List each alternative choice in the spaces labeled Choice I, II and III. For example, your three choices may be "change jobs"; "work part-time"; and "keep same job". (Of course, you may have more than three choices). Draw up your own balance sheet in that case. Also look again at your PSI to see the alternatives you listed as possible means to relieve your stresses. These alternatives could be just the choices for this chart.

Now evaluate how each of the choices affect the "lifestyle items" on the left side of the page. Use the following evaluation scale:

Very Negative	Negative	Neutral	Positive	Very Positive
-2	-1	0	1	2

Under each choice write down the number indicating how each of your lifestyle items will be affected by the choice.

Lifestyle Items

I. Family and Significant Others
   a. spouse or lover
   b. parents
   c. children
   d. friends
   e. colleagues
   f. the community
   g. other (list them)

II. Career
   a. financial situation
   b. your interest in the work
   c. chances for promotion
   d. creative challenge
   e. security
   f. free time
   g. status
   h. other (list them)

III. Self Considerations
   a. your personal values
   b. your moral standards
   c. contribution to community
      or society
   d. control over your life
   e. self image
   f. prestige
   g. gut feelings
   h. environment
   i. stress level
   j. health
   k. other (list them)

IV. Life Goals
   a. achievement of long
      range objectives
   b. pursuit of happiness
   c. retirement

When you complete the chart add all the numbers for each choice. The one with the highest sum is clearly the preferred change to make. Now, ask yourself this question: "Is this really the direction I want my life to take?" Look back over your answers to see if you "fudged" any of them to get the choice you think you wanted. Once you know for sure that all the evaluations are true and correct, your course of action is truly clear. Will you take the next step to change your life. That's up to you... and only you. No one can do it for you.

One way to help you put that new choice into action is to make a "contract" with yourself. Make it formal on a piece of paper. Give yourself a reward for completing the contract and a penalty for failing. For instance, your contract may read:

"Within six months from the date of this contract I will have found a job that gets me out of my 9 to 5 routine. The new job will not be in a stuffy office surrounded by smokers.

Upon finding this job I will join the health center I've always wanted to use, but never had enough time. If I do not find the job within six months, I will stop watching my favorite TV program and will no longer eat desserts with my meals."

Sign the contract, date it, and put it in a folder in a safe place. Now get going. You've only got six months!

Dealing With Job Stress

If left unchecked, job related stresses and strain can take a severe toll on your health and productivity. Follow some of these recommendations to help yourself survive in the sometimes hostile environment of the workplace.

Be Prepared. Go to work every day ready to do the best job that you possibly can. When you're given a task to do, always produce your highest quality work and try to finish on time. Don't wait until the last minute to complete assignments. Deadline pressures add to your stress, inhibit your creativity, and can reduce the overall quality of your work. As a rule, try to complete major projects a few days before they are due so you have adequate time to review them and make any necessary corrections.

Be Punctual. Make it a habit to arrive at appointments a few minutes early. Punctuality will add to your credibility and reduce your stress by eliminating the anxiety and physical stress responses that occur when you are constantly late.

Know What is Expected of You. It is essential that you know and understand the scope and responsibilities of your job. Stress occurs when you don't have a clear picture of: who you report to and who reports to you; what your specific duties are; the limits of your authority; and the criteria used to evaluate your performance. If your job has recently changed or has never been clearly defined, ask your supervisor or manager to provide you with a written, up-to-date job description.

<u>Be a Team Member</u>. If possible, treat your colleagues as teammates whose major goal is the same as yours: to win for your organization. Unfortunately, many negative things occur in the workplace (such as jealousy, deceit, backstabbing, lying, personality clashes, idea stealing, and power coalitions) that prevent feelings of team camaraderie. If you're experiencing these problems, here's some suggestions to help you improve your work relationships:

Be sensitive to the feelings and needs of your colleagues. They may return the courtesy. Never talk derisively about your fellow workers. If you do, they'll probably do the same to you. Essentially, treat others as you want to be treated.

Try to be courteous and friendly, but always maintain a professional approach towards work. Keep your private life out of the workplace. Think twice before getting involved with someone at the office. In addition, never trust anyone at work with a secret. Even best friends have been known to break confidences if they can personally gain. Secrets are ammunition your enemies can use against you.

Confront negativity and hostility in your colleagues. If you perceive that a serious communication barrier exists between yourself and a co-worker and you don't know what is causing it, confront the individual directly. Come right out and ask the person questions such as: "What have I done to you? Why are you being so hostile towards me? What can we do to eliminate this problem?" Getting personality conflicts out in the open as soon as possible keeps the work environment from becoming an unfriendly battleground. Although some people may never be able to work together comfortably, an uneasy coexistence is better than a high degree of work-related stress.

<u>Stand Up For Your Rights</u>. When you are unfairly blamed for a problem, don't sit back and take the abuse passively. If someone slanders you for no apparent reason, first get to the root of the problem. Gather all the facts of the situation, then tactfully and unemotionally present your side of the story to your supervisor. Dealing with this sort of problem as soon as possible will minimize its impact on your mind, body, and overall stress level.

<u>Maintain Your Integrity</u>. At times, some employers ask you to do things that go against your values and better judgement. If you refuse an

assignment on moral grounds, you risk losing your job but maintaining your self-esteem; if you neglect your true feelings, you risk losing your self-respect. You do have a choice. If your job frequently compromises your integrity, change jobs.

Relax at Noon. If you're having a very trying day, go for a brisk walk at lunchtime or do some stretching and focused breathing. These activities burn off excess tension and help take your mind off the problems. You can also try sitting in your car or in a private quiet room at the office and listen to a relaxation tape or self improvement tape.

Avoid or Restructure High Stress Positions. Some jobs have a tendency to kill the people that hold them. Today it costs so much to replace and retrain key employees who succumb to stress-related illnesses that it behooves companies to hire organizational development specialists to restructure these positions.

GENERAL STRESS REDUCTION TIPS

1. The best way to reduce your stress is to enjoy your life.

2. Take control and responsibility for yourself. Direct your energies on the path that best fulfills your needs, wants, aspirations, and goals, while allowing for your pursuit of happiness.

3. Don't live to fulfill someone else's expectations.

4. Your mind and the body are one, so incorporate activities in your life that tone the body and calm the mind.

5. Love and pamper yourself.

6. Keep learning and growing.

7. Keep a positive attitude; have confidence in your abilities and avoid negative thinking. Don't belittle yourself. If you keep saying negative things about yourself, you'll eventually begin to believe them.

8. Take time to relax and think your own thoughts. It's unhealthy to constantly be preoccupied with work or your problems. Let your

mind have a rest by giving it a chance to think about fun and beauty. Enjoy your time off and don't feel guilty about it. You deserve it. When you come home from work, take a shower, put on relaxing clothes, and separate yourself from the tension of the day.

9. Participate each week in at least three aerobic exercise sessions that maintain your heart rate in your target range for at least twenty minutes. Exercise and deep relaxation are the cheapest, most effective health insurance available.

10. Try to practice some techniques of deep relaxation for at least twenty minutes, three times a week. Deep relaxation is productive time that will help you perform your job more effectively.

11. Each day, perform a few quick exercises for improving your posture, breathing and flexibility.

12. Try to get 6-8 hours of sleep each night.

13. Eat a well balanced diet avoiding caffeine, salt, sugar, grease, too much fat and cholesterol, artificial flavoring and coloring, and junk food.

14. If you have a drug or alcohol problem, get professional help. You may have to change your life (and your circle of "friends") but it's in your best interest that you sober up.

15. Participate in hobbies that keep you physically active. Being a couch potato does not count.

16. Don't try to relax when you have a lot to do. Get your work done first. When you finish, sit back and completely enjoy your relaxation. You've earned it.

17. Be productive without killing yourself. Set attainable goals that help achieve your long range objectives. Reward yourself when you succeed.

18. Modify your behavior or life by making the changes that reduce your stress.

132

19. Don't exaggerate the importance of your problems. In the whole scheme of things many problems are actually inconsequential.

20. Enjoy your life as you did when you were a child. Remember how to play and laugh and enjoy special moments to their fullest.

Suggested Relaxation Tapes and
Stress Reducing Products

o Environmental sounds by Syntonic Research, Inc., 175 Fifth
   Avenue, New York, NY 10010:

   SC99001   Slow Ocean
   SC99002   Ultimate Thunderstorm
   SC99003   Sailboat
   SC99011   English Meadow
   SC99022   Crickets

o The music of Steven Halpern

o The music of Paul Horn

o Relaxation tapes by Dr. Jeffrey Forman, including:

   Focused Breathing

   Work Day Relaxation Training

   Pain and Headache Relief

   Postural Realignment - a stretching, breathing, and
   deep relaxation program

   Sleep Improvement

   Improving Your Creativity

For information on how to purchase natural curve neck pillows, cervical
traction pillows, back cushions, and Dr. Forman's relaxation tapes, write
to:

   Stress Reduction Systems
   P.O. Box 24263
   San Jose, CA 95154-4263

For information on how to order inexpensive biofeedback equipment, write
to:

   Stens Corporation
   Department JF
   6451 Oakwood Drive
   Oakland, CA 94611

The Publisher offers discounts on this book when ordered in
bulk quantities. For more information write:

   Special Sales/College Marketing
   Prentice-Hall, Inc.
   College Book Division
   Englewood Cliffs, New Jersey 07632
   (201)592-2498

Druker, Peter F., Management, New York: Harper and Row, 1974

Ferrucci, Piero, What We May Be: Techniques For Psychological and Spiritual Growth Through Psychosynthesis, J.P. Tarcher, Inc., Los Angeles, California, 1982

Funt, Lawrence A. D.D.S. M.S., A New Approach to Chronic Headache, The Female Patient, Vol. 51, May 1980 p. 28-33

Goldberg, Philip, Executive Health, New York: McGraw Hill, 1978

Goldberg, Philip and Daniel Kaufman, Natural Sleep: How To Get Your Share, Rodale Press, Emmaus, PA, 1978

Kahn, R.L., Et.Al., Occupational Stress, Springfield, Illinois: Charles C. Thomas, 1974

Kendall, Henry O., P.T., Florence Picendall P.T. and Gladys T. Wadsworth, P.T., MUSCLES: Testing and Function, Second Edition, The Williams and Wilkins Company, Baltimore, 1971

Lust, John, The Herb Book, Benedict Lust Publications, Sini Valley, California, 1974

Maxmen, Jerrold S., M.D., A Good Night's Sleep - A Step by Step Program for Overcoming Insomnia and Other Sleep Problems, W.W. Norton and Company, New York, 1981

Naranjo, Claudio and Robert E. Ornstein, On the Psychology of Meditation, New York: Warner Destiny Books, 1977

Patterson, Ann, Acupressure Workbook, c Ann Patterson, San Francisco, California, 1981

Prudden, Bonnie, Pain Erasure, the Bonnie Prudden Way, M. Evans and Company, Inc., New York, 1980

Taylor, Paul L. and Bruce M. Bongar, Clinical Applications in Biofeedback Therapy, Los Angeles: Psychology Press, 1976

Williams, Marian and Catherine Worthingham, Therapeutic EXERCISE: For Body Alignment and Function, W.B. Saunders Company, Philadelphia, Pennsylvania, 1957

Pelletier, Kenneth R., Mind as Healer, Mind As Slayer, New York: Dell Co., Inc., 1977

Rama, S., Et. Al, Science of Breath: A Practical Guide, Honsdale, Pennsylvania: The Himalayan International Institute of Yoga Science and Philosophy, 1979

Abdominal strengthening 57-58
Activities to avoid 38-39
Acupressure
  explanation of 96
  directions for 97, 100-103, 108
Acupressure Charts
  common sore points 101
  headache relief points 108
  side of head and neck points 102
  sole of foot points 105
Aerobic exercise
  benefits 37
  cautions 38
  recommendations 40-41
  training tips 41-42
Alcohol
  and diet 115
  sleep impairment 82-83, 87
Auditory detachment 77-78
Autogenic training 72-73, 109

Back care 53-59
  abdominal strengthening 57-58
  activities to avoid 38-39
  acupressure 100-101
  back cushions 103, 134
  gluteal (seat muscle)
    strengthening 59
  heat 92-94
  hip flexor stretches 54
  ice 95
  ideal sleeping position 86
  low back stretches 55-56
  massage 96-105
  mattresses 84-85
  pelvic alignment 53
  relieving pain 92-103
  supplemental tips 59
Back cushions 103, 134
Biofeedback
  anxiety syndrome 106-107
  Burger's disease 106-107
  diabetes 106-107
  hand warming 106-107
  headache relief 106-107
  high blood pressure 106-107
  muscle relaxation 73, 106
  Raynaud's disease 106-107
Breathing
  basic exercises 33-34
  common faults 33
  focused exercises 34-36
  for relaxation 33-36
  proper mechanics of 31-32

Calf stretches 67-68
Caffeine 113
  and sleep 87
Cardio-vascular
  conditioning 40-42
  problems 120

Decision Making 127-129
Diet
  amino acids 112
  caffeine 87, 113
  cholesterol and fat 114-115
  digestive problems or ulcers 120
  fiber 113
  general tips 113-117
  HDL & LDLs 115
  health risk self appraisal 117-121
  heart disease (cardiovascular
    problems) 120
  herbs 88
  high blood pressure 120
  ideal body fat 112
  minor illness and fatigue 121
  muscle spasms 88, 120
  salt 114
  sleep improvement 87-88, 120
  sugar 114
  to reduce stress 87, 113-117
  vitamins 116-117

Exercises
  abdominal strengthening 57-58
  aerobic training tips 41-42
  breathing 33-34
  calf flexibility 67-68
  eye exercises 109-110
  gluteal (seat muscle)
    strengthening 59
  hamstring flexibility 64-65
  hip flexibility 63
  hip flexor stretches 54
  low back problems 54-59
  low back stretches 55-56
  neck realignment 45-47
  posture realignment 45-60
  round shoulders 49-52
  safe 60-69
  shoulder flexibility 60-63
  thigh (quadriceps)
    flexibility 66-67
  to avoid 38-39
  training heart rate 40-41
  trunk rotation 59-60
  recommendations 40
  routine development 69

INDEX (cont'd)